CONCISE
HANDBOOK FOR
NEW MANAGERS

The Scott, Foresman Applications
in Management Series

ROBERT B. NELSON, *Editor*

CONCISE HANDBOOK FOR NEW MANAGERS

Brad Lee Thompson

SCOTT, FORESMAN AND COMPANY

Glenview, Illinois   London

Library of Congress Cataloging-in-Publication Data

Thompson, Brad Lee.
   Concise handbook for new managers / Brad Lee
Thompson.
      p.   cm. — (The Scott, Foresman applications in
  management series)
   ISBN 0-673-38952-9
   1. Management — Handbooks, manuals, etc.
I. Title. II. Series.
  HD31.T4887   1990
658.4—dc20   89-70008
                                      CIP

1 2 3 4 5 6 RRC 94 93 92 91 90 89

ISBN 0-673-38952-9

Scott, Foresman professional books are available for bulk
sales at quantity discounts. For information, please
contact Marketing Manager, Professional Books Group,
Scott, Foresman and Company, 1900 East Lake Avenue,
Glenview, IL 60025.

Series Foreword

The Scott, Foresman Applications in Management Series provides short, practical, easy-to-read books about basic business skills.

Low on theory and high on practical techniques and examples, this series addresses the key skill areas needed to be a successful manager in business today. It supplies specific answers to questions you have and offers new approaches to problems you face in your job.

Each book in the series is written by one or more individuals who have extensive, first-hand experience in the topic being discussed. The drafted books are then reviewed by several front-line managers to ensure that each meets their needs in delivering practical, useful information in a format that is easy to understand and use.

I am confident that this book—and others in the AIM series—will provide you with tips and techniques to enable you to do your job better today and in the future.

Robert B. Nelson
Series Editor

Contents

1

Making the Change from Worker to Manager

Yesterday, you were one of the group. Today, you're the boss. Congratulations on your promotion!

Take a moment to catch your breath and give yourself some credit. You must be doing a lot of good work. Your managers obviously believe they are doing the right thing for the company by putting you in charge.

Now you have some choices to make: What kind of boss are you going to be? How are you going to change our relationships with the people with whom you used to work as peers? Also, you've probably declared more than once that there are better ways to run the company; now that you're in charge, which of your ideas are you going to act on first?

WHAT AM I GETTING MYSELF INTO?

What's that? You say you're not sure you want to be a manager?

Your anxiety is understandable. Until now, your view of management has probably been somewhat one-sided. Maybe you have even had first-hand experience with managers who were difficult to work for because they

- gave lots of orders and rarely listened to new ideas,
- said little about what was going on elsewhere in the company,
- failed to plan well, which meant you had to work evenings or on weekends,
- provided confusing feedback about your performance,
- generally did not support your efforts to do your job.

Do you recognize anyone you know? Your list could probably go on and on. It is a fact of life that some managers are more effective than others. If you have suffered with a poor manager, you already know a lot about what NOT to do. It's no wonder you are a little anxious: No one wants to be a poor manager—ineffective and causing unhappiness among those who work for him.

But it doesn't have to be so. Being a manager can be an immensely satisfying experience for you and for those who work for you. By managing the efforts of others, you have more opportunities to make your ideas come to life. You can be a leader, a mentor, a person of vision and action who is respected and rewarded for your contributions to the bottom line and quality of work life in the company.

Being a manager doesn't suit everyone, but successful new managers give the following reasons why it was worthwhile for them to give up their comfortable, familiar jobs to become managers:

1. *Managers can grow, personally and professionally.*   Change can be uncertain and at times uncomfortable, but otherwise sane and healthy people like you are attracted to the management ranks because they believe they are ready to learn something new, do a new job, and practice new skills.

2. *Managers can make more of a difference.*   Being a manager means having a voice that is listened to by those above and below in the organization. Generally, the higher a person moves in the organization, the more he or she can affect the success of the organization.

3. *Managers get more rewards.*   Greater rewards come with greater contributions to the success of the organization. Some rewards are financial, some are preferential like a reserved parking space, and some are psychological, such as the satisfaction for having met a new challenge successfully.

What does it really mean to be a manager? Your experience will be unique, of course. The job will probably be more tedious than you expected, harder than you imagined, and almost certainly without the dreamed-of glamor and power. You will have to get used to the idea that you are getting paid to have difficult conversations with people, and you will be amazed that you have to talk to them about everything from their poor performance to their offensive hygiene!

You will be disappointed to find that you cannot change the organization overnight. You may become discouraged when you have to live with contradictions, paradoxes, and unresolved situations. And you may find yourself perpetually frustrated with office politics, pointless meetings, bureaucratic pettiness, indecision from above and below, shifting priorities, and chronic lack of time and resources.

You may even discover that you were promoted for the wrong reasons. It may not matter as much as you think that you have been successful so far because you work hard, contribute consistently, and have demonstrated a commitment to the organization and its values. The fact that you are a good worker, a seasoned employee who knows the routines, or a nice person may have little bearing on your future success as a manager. Superior sales people do not always make good sales managers, and an excellent staff worker may be a mediocre staff leader. Managing requires you to learn new skills, adopt a broader perspective, make deeper commitments.

So can YOU be a successful manager? Maybe. You have quite a bit going for you already because you have the confidence of your managers; in their opinion, you have what is required to be successful. Your work so far has met their expectations.

You also have your recent work experience working in your favor. Because you know first-hand the problems and conditions out on the line, you are in an excellent position to remedy the problems.

In addition, you have this book. The no-nonsense coaching found herein will help you to anticipate the challenges you will face, to solve specific problems along the way, and, most of all, to keep things in perspective.

I LIKE AND RESPECT MY FRIENDS. NOW THAT I'M THEIR BOSS, WHAT SHOULD I EXPECT?

Expect the best, but be prepared for some lingering resentment and occasional tests of your authority. Nancy Adams, a new marketing manager, heard the following comments from her former peers within the first few days after her promotion; notice how Nancy responded:

Employee: "Congratulations, Nancy—you're going to be great!"

Nancy: "Thank you! I think we're ALL going to be a great team!"

Employee: "I'm glad they finally put someone in charge who knows what it's like out in the field. Can we get new dealer sales kits now?"

Nancy: "I don't know yet—but I know it's important to you, so it's going to be one of the first concerns I address. I'll let you know by next week."

Employee: "I don't like the new compensation plan, Nancy. And you wouldn't like it either, if you weren't a supervisor now."

Nancy: "Do you think I'm suddenly a different person now? I have never automatically agreed with you or anyone else in the past. Remember the new cooperative advertising program? I told you then I thought you were wrong. I'm an individual, and I bring my own ideas, values, and experiences to this job."

Employee: "Look, I resent you—you're younger than I am, and I have more experience. I always thought of you as a friend, but I can see now that you're just like everybody else— just looking out for number one."

Nancy: "I'm sorry you feel that way. You know I've earned this promotion. When you are less upset, I hope we can talk about this differently. I still regard you as a valuable member of the team, and we'll still need you to achieve our goals. Think this over, and let's talk tomorrow."

People who were once your co-workers may have feelings of resentment or envy toward you because of your promotion. They will also have concerns, such as what your new position will mean for them and their careers.

You may lose some friends. If you used to work with the people you are now supervising, you can expect some awkward moments. Some people may try to take advantage of your new position; if they perceive you as their "friend at the top," you may be expected to look the other way when rules are bent, to grant special favors, and to generally make their lives easier. If you are supervising a group of people with whom you are not famililar, you can expect to be tested. In either case, prepare to prove yourself after a short honeymoon period.

NOW THAT I AM MANAGER, WHAT ELSE IS DIFFERENT?

1. *Your job is to get the expected results from your work group.* Before you became a supervisor, your responsibility was limited to the tasks you personally performed. You probably did not have to lose sleep when someone in your department did not do their job (unless, of course, you were the one assigned to work overtime to make it right).

   Now, your chief responsibility is to see that all the work of your department gets done and done properly. YOU must plan and organize the resources to accomplish the objectives of your work group, and YOU must hold yourself accountable for your work group's results. It is your job to help everyone else complete their work successfully—and to assign the overtime if they don't! You do this by

a. learning much more about your company's goals and understanding how your department contributes to those goals,

b. setting and communicating the priorities that guide your work team's day-to-day activities,

c. developing and implementing good work plans that get the work finished on time and within budget,

d. ,providing direction and feedback to your coworkers about their job performance.

2. *You see the "big picture."* You now look at the company with a wider view, a broader perspective. The word *supervision* comes from the Latin, "to see over, to see from above." This is the management point of view you share with other managers.

Rather than focusing on an isolated bit of work activity, you are concerned with "big picture" questions: What work is in progress? What do we have to do to get ready for it? Who is doing what, and will they finish on time? What resources can we commit to solving the quality problems that came up in the employee meeting? Is the department within its budget? Can we improve productivity by buying new equipment, or would we save more time by changing the way we process finished parts?

Looking at the big picture does not free you from details. On the contrary, details about production, materials costs, scheduling, budgets, and many other subroutines are important pieces of the management puzzle.

Sometimes working with the smallest details provides the clues with which you can solve the big problems. But details can be seductive time traps. They can create the illusion of making progress simply because they make you feel busy. For example, to spend three days evaluating software may be a necessary exercise for you, or it may be a waste of your time because it is a task that could and should be delegated.

You must learn to think critically about problems and opportunities in ways that make the best use of your company's time and money. You must learn to make wise choices about where you direct your efforts. Almost always, your time is better spent thinking about options—the big picture—while your people think about details.

3. *You must work through others.* Your ideas and plans can never be realized unless and until you have the support of your work team. In turn, you must support their efforts by being the best manager you can be. This almost always means you must spend more time delegating and directing and less time doing. You simply cannot assume the time-consuming tasks of managing without giving up the work you used to do. This is hard.

If you used to earn your pay as a millwright or a computer programmer, for example, you are likely to be frustrated with less capable people reporting to you in those positions. You will be tempted to involve yourself in their work because you know it so well. Wouldn't it take less time just to roll up your sleeves, wade into the problems, and fix everything yourself?

Sure, it would be faster—today. But it would be better for the overall success of the company tomorrow if your work team learned to do their jobs without depending on you to save the day. Your challenge is to cause them to depend on you less and depend on themselves more. Probably, they would let you do their jobs and even let you feel like a hero (why wouldn't they?) but what does that really gain for you and for the company in the long run?

You can help your people learn their jobs better by stepping back and letting them make their own decisions, even if they sometimes make mistakes that cost the company money. This is the best on-the-job training they can get. Don't become a manager who doesn't have time to manage because he's doing everyone else's job. Besides, who knows? Maybe the millwrights or computer programmers reporting to you will come up with some new solutions to old problems. Your experience and know-how are most valuable to the company when you *supervise,* not when you do the work. Try getting out of the way so your workers can do their jobs—and then go and do yours!

4. *You get and give more information.* You now communicate with more people, more often. You cannot be isolated or insulated. It's

your job to know what is going on and to tell your people what is going on, so that everyone can do their work together smoothly.

In most organizations, information is the currency of power. The more you know, the more power you are perceived to have. Corporate mythology says that to share information is to give up power. Actually, the reverse is true: When you share information with your work group, you empower them to contribute more to achieving your department's objectives. Then, when the department succeeds, everyone succeeds.

One of your most difficult tasks is to build and manage your information channels. An opportune time to ask all kinds of questions is while you are still new to the job. (See those listed in Fig. A-2 in Appendix A.)

Some workers in your work group may give you too much information because they want to impress you with their accomplishments or campaign for their favorite project. Other workers may be reluctant to share what they know because they do not believe in empowerment. Further complicating your communication will be the blizzard of memos, correspondence, and trade journals landing on your desk. You are wondering what is really important, what information needs to be passed on to others. What other information are you *not* receiving and need to go out and get? Is everyone learning what they need to know? Are you getting an accurate understanding of what's going on around you?

How can you be sure your information channels are uncluttered, quick, and reliable? A quick way to check is to ask yourself: Is anyone getting surprised? Few surprises in business are pleasant. Surprises are symptoms of unclear or incomplete communication. If you, your workers, or your boss receive one too many nasty surprises, exercise your managerial authority to get more of the right information.

5. *You solve problems.* Better yet, you now anticipate potential problems and dismantle them before they cost time and money to fix. Among managers, this is called "getting in front of the snowball" in order to stop it before it rolls downhill, out of control, getting bigger all the time. You are no longer a bystander; now you are paid to solve and prevent problems.

6. *You work with other managers.* You have a new set of peers now: other managers. Together, you comprise the leadership of the company. You need to support each other in a variety of ways.

Mark Gordon stumbled into an awkward situation with another member of the management team after he had been a supervisor for about two months. Here's what he was hearing from his workers:

Employee: "Mark, the supervisor of the other department is not as strict as you are. They do not have to make up time when they come in late or leave early or take a long lunch hour. You're nitpicking about a few minutes here and there."

Mark was stumped for a good response: "I don't know what to say. I'm following company policy. All I can say is that I'll talk to Marie in the other department."

Employee: "We want to do it their way. As it is, we think the situation is unfair."

Later, Mark was very direct with Marie: "Your relaxed policy about checking in and out is causing me problems. I'm on the verge of a mutiny over there, and the productivity of my people is on the downslide. Why aren't you enforcing company policy?"

Marie smiled: "Mark, I believe that getting the job done is more important than just rigidly enforcing a policy. Yes, I admit I'm bending the rules. But here's why: Most of my workers are seasoned employees who know their jobs better than I ever will. I've relaxed this rule as a way to acknowledge their experience and show the company's trust and respect. They know they have earned my trust: I trust them to always get their jobs done. They also know that the consequence for poor performance will be a stricter check-in and check-out policy."

Mark: "But can't you tell them compliance with this policy is part of their job description? Can't you just tell them to do it or find another job?"

Marie: "That would be a bit extreme, wouldn't it? Do you know how important these people are to our success as a company? You can't easily replace trained people like these. I'm not going to change my approach on this. It's taken a long time to get to this point. In my judgment, these people deserve to be treated like adults who do their jobs well. I don't allow any excesses or abuses of my relaxed policy, but I'm not going to become a clockwatcher, either."

Mark found Marie's logic compelling. Her department *did* have excellent performance and good morale. But what could he do? He worried that his workers were less experienced and considerably younger. He decided that he would share Marie's approach with his workers. Perhaps if they understood the responsibilities assumed by Marie's department, a relaxed policy could work for their department, too, in time. At the very least, he would demonstrate that he was sincerely trying to be fair.

Mark learned two lessons from this experience. First, his success depends on the cooperation and aid of other managers as much as of his workers. Second, the best policies are the policies that get the job done.

7. *Finally, you are one of many partners in the success of the business.* Now you are all

resources for each other in the enterprise. You are in partnership with your new manager and other senior managers. You are in partnership with your peers, workers, and even your vendors. In a real sense, your new job is to collaborate with your partners so you can all work together for the success of the business.

WHAT MAKES A MANAGER SUCCESSFUL?

Now that you have some understanding of what a manager is and what a manager does, let's explore why some managers succeed and others fail.

A manager is considered successful when performance or results meet or exceed expectations. If you ask a dozen successful managers the reasons for their success, you'll get different answers that may sound something like this:

"I am successful because I routinely ask and answer the three most important questions for a manager:
What's *really* going on here?
What is the most important task for me to be doing now?
What can I finish today?"

"When your work group succeeds, you succeed—so you do whatever it takes to help your people succeed."

"Dumb luck and smart luck. First, you have to be—or get to be—in the right place at the right time. Then, you work like hell to make the most of the opportunity."

"Teamwork."

"Planning."

"Making more right decisions than wrong decisions. And never, never make three big mistakes in a row."

"Leadership."

"Learning the difference between the 'nice to do' work and the 'need to do' work. Do the important stuff first."

"Reserve your passion for results. Do not become so heavily invested in an idea or approach that you cannot see when it should be dropped."

"When you're wrong, admit it and move on."

Actually, all these and more contribute to a manager's success. But no one approach or set of skills solves every problem.

Learning to manage really means learning to exercise sound judgment and to make good decisions. Successful management is a series of decisions that leads to the accomplishment of the organization's objectives. It's not as simple as sorting the right decisions from the wrong decisions because your options are rarely simply right or simply wrong.

Management requires you to use your best judgment and common sense to choose the trade-offs that will best support the organization after all the options are considered. In our earlier example what was better for Mark Gordon—to relax the rules, to enforce the company's policy, to change Marie's approach, or to ignore the problem altogether? Mark's choices affected everyone who worked for him. Like Mark, you have to appreciate the fact that your decisions affect everyone who works for you. From now on, your choices influence the success of others.

We can control, or at least affect, our successes and failures through the decisions we make. You understand this already as it relates to your personal life; you must have done enough things right to earn your promotion!

Consider what failure can teach us about success. Failures terrify us as much as successes thrill us. Like our successes, our failures look and feel different to each of us: getting fired, being passed over for promotion, wasting an opportunity, blowing the budget, losing a valuable employee, being reassigned to a dead-end job.

How do you deal with your personal failures now? Do you try to cover them up, deny they ever happened, pretend they aren't important? You know you can't. As a manager, you are too visible to get away with that kind of self-deception.

You *must* understand that most of your failures are of your own making. You cannot learn from mistakes until you acknowledge them for what they are. New managers are especially vulnerable to the myth that they are not allowed to fail. Is this realistic? Which of your senior managers has never failed, suffered a setback, or made a mistake?

You naturally want to prove yourself, to reinforce the decision to promote you, but you don't have the luxury of self-deception any longer. Your peers and partners on the management team need your view of reality, not your wish list. If you admit your mistakes and learn from them, your judgment will continue to improve. Next time, better decisions are likely to yield better performance.

Do you see how failures are linked to our choices, too? The quality of our decision-making always shows up in performance. Did we—our work group or our organization—do our job? Poor judgment leads to poor performance, and poor performance leads to negative consequences. Better judgment means better results, more successes, and fewer failures.

The steps of the corporate ladder occasionally become too slippery for nearly everyone. You, too, can expect to have your share of trips and slips if you continue to climb it. A recent survey of 191 male and female managers who were from large companies and who considered themselves successful revealed that they had almost all suffered "hardship experiences," including missed promotions, firings, and business failures.

Each of these managers bounced back from failure. To them, failure was part of the growth process and was the logical outcome of one or more bad decisions. Failure did not mean that they were bad people. The Center for Creative Leadership, a research firm in Greensboro, North Carolina, which was the survey coordinator, discovered that these successful managers shared a willingness to accept responsibility for causing their failure. Rather than blame others, they admitted their mistakes and moved on, sometimes to new jobs, new employers, or new careers. Here are five of the most common causes of self-induced failure identified by the managers:

1. *They are unable to get along.* Poor interpersonal skills cause most managers most of their problems. They don't listen enough, they don't share enough information, and they fail to treat subordinates with respect.

> The program leader at a large computer firm referred to a former colleague who had just taken a position with another company this way: "We're glad she's gone. She made happy-talk with us, then asked us—no, told us—to help her do her job. She doesn't have a family, but we do. The marathon phone calls at home, the routine weekend work . . . she drove the staff crazy. She was proud of the fact that she received new assignments every year or so—frankly, I think that's about the time it took to burn out her staffs. Maybe senior management appreciated her ability to get things done, but I don't think they saw the walking wounded she left behind."

Arrogance, disrespect, and other unpleasant attitudes lead to predictable results: alienation, lack of trust, high turnover, and poor morale. And the problems are not limited to subordinates; some managers continue to have problems with their peers and bosses, too.

2. *They fail to adapt.* Sometimes the ideal fit between a talented person and an organization is stretched to the breaking point when the

business, the person, the industry, or the market changes.

An employed manager complained bitterly: "I helped start this division. They needed someone like me who could do the open-field running, make decisions on the fly, think fast and respond on a moment's notice—oh, what's the use? They've all gone corporate now. I predict they'll blow it within the year."

What was valued in a manager at one time—new ideas or forthright discussion, for example—may not be appreciated forever. A manager's style, priorities, focus of energy, industry, and company knowledge have to stay up-to-date and continue to match the organization.

3. *They are trapped in the "me only" syndrome.* Managers preoccupied with how much recognition they are getting eventually find themselves alone, even though they may make significant contributions on their way up the corporate ladder.

Manager: "It was tough toward the end. I actually got to the point where I was doing things because they were good for me, not because they were good for the company. Our agendas used to be the same, but somewhere along the way I began behaving as if the company was there to serve my needs, not the other way around. If I were them, I would have fired me, too.''

''Me only'' managers have trouble leading others and setting their own needs aside for the company's needs. They are hard to work for because they are not authentic team players.

4. *They are afraid to act.* One way to avoid failure, some managers reason, is to avoid making risky decisions and delay taking risky actions. In other words, make yourself a smaller target for criticism by keeping a very low profile. These managers may actually be hard workers who otherwise contribute good ideas, but they lack the commitment or the courage to move their ideas and plans forward. ''Paralysis because of analysis'' or ''playing it too safe'' summarizes their problem. Their inability to come to closure actually puts them at greater risk.

Example: A since-departed manager actually took more than a year to study the performance appraisal system and make revisions. He looked busy all that time, but by the time he finished, the department had a whole new staff, including a new manager, and they were happily using a totally different system!

5. *They are unable to rebound.* The Center for Creative Leadership's study found that a

manager's ability to recover after a setback was crucial to his or her ultimate success.

Heard in the sauna at the health club:

"I'd still be on my way up if those imports hadn't ruined the market!"

"It was office politics, plain and simple—you wouldn't believe what the Dragon Lady did to me!"

"Sure, I've had a setback or two, but who hasn't? This thing was a fluke. I'm just going to get back on that horse and ride it again—see, I'm persistent, maybe even stubborn. And I'll keep doing it until my ship comes in; you can bank on that."

Managers who seem to be dogged by failure actually cause more problems for themselves because they react to failure by becoming defensive, trying to conceal their failures, or blaming others for their misfortunes. These managers have narrow, brittle definitions of success for themselves that require excessive rationalization as protection from the real world. Successful managers, on the other hand, are resilient. They admit their mistakes, learn their lessons, and strive to do better next time. Because most careers tend to zigzag upward, "the ability to handle failures well can make or break a climb to the top," according to the study of the Center for Creative Leadership.

So, what *does* make a manager successful? It sounds so easy: The successful manager sees to it that the right work gets done in the right way at the right time. To do this, he or she incorporates the corporate priorities and values into a rational decision-making process called good judgment. The successful manager accepts accountability for the good, bad, or mediocre accomplishments of his or her work group. It is never easy and not always fair, but no one ever guaranteed that it would be, did they?

CAN I BE A SUCCESSFUL MANAGER?

Sure. It's not brain surgery. And you have this book to help you get started. The basics we'll cover here will provide the foundation for your future development—not a moment invested in yourself with this book will be wasted time. It gets you off on the right foot, fast—then keeps you moving forward, one problem at a time, in roughly the sequence you'll encounter them.

In the following chapters, we'll describe in detail what a manager does, why it's important, and how to do it well. We'll also examine the nature of your relationships with your workers, and develop guidelines for keeping them productive and healthy. We'll look at the good and bad sides of power, communication that works, and the management and measurement of performance. Finally, we'll troubleshoot people problems you're likely to encounter and your challenge to continue your development.

Do you still want to be a manager? It's your choice. Only you can decide if this assignment rewards you well enough to continue. Sometimes you'll love your new job; other times you'll wish you were back on the line with your buddies where life was a lot simpler.

The reluctant manager is a poor manager, so if you choose to proceed, decide to do the best you can do. The world does not need another half-hearted, mediocre manager!

"Until there is commitment, there is always ineffectiveness."
Goethe

2

The Manager's Roles

Mark Gordon's second week on the job is going poorly. He is talking with Janice, a staff person from the human resources department.

Mark: "What do you mean I have to rehire Jeff? I caught him with illegal drugs in the restroom. I fired him for breaking the law—and if I can't do that, you'd better tell me what I *can* do, because I'm *very* confused."

Janice wants to help Mark. She understands his frustration. She does not want to dampen his energy and enthusiasm for his new supervisory job, but he has overstepped his limits this time.

Janice: "Mark, you can't just fire a person. It may be simple from your point of view, but there's a right way and a wrong way."

Mark: "You mean there is a slow way and a no way, don't you? He's been pulling this stuff for a long time. Remember, I know that crew like they're my family. I *know* Jeff is a threat to himself and everyone else back there . . ."

Janice: "I appreciate how you feel, but you—meaning the company—can't make this stick. *If* he has a problem . . ."

Mark: "I can't believe what I'm hearing. Please explain to me how he can get away with this and still keep his job."

Janice: "Well, first of all, you are not qualified to diagnose a drug problem—at least not in the eyes of the law. Second, even if you called the police to arrest him, AND even if we cooperated with them to catch Jeff in the act, he's entitled to due process in the courts. Also, arresting him doesn't automatically mean he loses his job. Furthermore, this company believes in a progressive disciplinary system, so Jeff is going to spend a lot of time with the employee assistance program to get drug education and treatment. Finally, he's a union employee, and he has an entire grievance and appeal process he can exercise."

Mark: "So we've got to take him back?"

Janice: "For now, with strict guidelines."

Mark was quiet for a moment. "I'm going to lose some credibility with the rest of the crew over this, aren't I?"

Janice: "I'm sorry. Good luck—next time."

Mark is learning the hard way that being a manager can be frustrating and confusing. Like you, Mark is learning that situations are not always so clear-cut as they were before he was promoted. You have probably bumped heads with someone by now over a similarly tough-to-resolve situation. Perhaps you, too, have been disappointed in some ways with decisions or trade-offs or compromises that someone else made for the greater good of the company. If you are bound by the company's labor contract, if the sales people can demand changes in your production schedule, or if senior management refuses to support your position on a contract dispute because of "political considerations," you naturally begin to wonder what your job is all about.

Just what role is the manager expected to play? Policeman? Leader? Babysitter? Coach? The manager used to be the guy who simply carried out the orders of his boss. The thinking, the deciding, and the responsibility resided at the top of the organization and flowed downward, just like in the military service. The junior manager was no more and no less than an extension of the senior manager.

The contemporary manager fulfills four basic roles: planner, organizer, influencer, and controller. To succeed in these roles, you must be a skilled communicator, decision maker, and problem solver. It would not hurt to be sensitive to corporate politics, either.

It is a fact of life that your job cannot be sharply focused. One manager put it this way: "If there's a problem, and no one else claims it, it ends up on my desk." If you are most comfortable following orders, you may find your new roles unsettling. If you are being told on Monday that you have the responsibility and authority to accomplish certain work, but then receive conflicting directions by Wednesday, you are going to be confused and frustrated.

Don't let yourself become discouraged or cynical. With time, you'll learn to recognize your limitations, your opportunities, and the difficult situations that you cannot do anything about. With a little help, you can learn to make your job the best it can be most of the time.

Despite the fact that there are aspects of your job you cannot control, you are not excused from doing your best. You know you have many positive contributions to make. This is your opportunity to grow, make a larger difference in the company, change employees' behaviors, and implement some of your new ideas! The sooner you become comfortable with your new roles, the happier you will be.

Before we examine your role as a planner, let's look at how your job has evolved.

MEET THE NEW MANAGER

Managers become necessary when businesses grow larger. In very small businesses, the people doing the work can often manage themselves because everyone knows what everyone else is doing. Small business owners commonly wear all the hats to get all the work done: production manager, sales manager, financial manager, and research and development manager. Each time a new person joins the organization, however, the work to be done becomes a little more fragmented, and communication becomes a little more complex. Soon, the company needs people who only manage.

This book describes all types of bosses—supervisors, chiefs, foremen, administrators, leadmen, department heads, district coordinators, and others—as managers. Each performs the four roles or functions of management: planning, organizing, influencing, and controlling. Over the years, these roles have remained the same, but *how* managers fulfilled these roles has continued to change.

It was not too long ago that a manager was expected to do his or her job "by the book." Policy or procedures manuals attempted to prescribe the actions to be taken and the decisions to be made for every situation the manager might face.

This dependence on policies and procedures was comforting as long as the manager was expected to carry out decisions made by someone else. The manuals were useful as long as there were only minimal changes from year to year. But as soon as the marketplace became more competitive, and as soon as new technologies changed the way people do business, managers' roles and responsibilities changed dramatically. Now, there isn't time to keep the procedures manuals up to date; they would be out of date before the revisions could be agreed upon.

Management has become a job requiring you to rely more on your judgment than on a policy or procedures manual. Don't panic: Your non-managerial experience has probably prepared you with an understanding of how your company functions day to day. Your common sense, your sense of the company's values and priorities, and your instincts about your fellow employees further enrich your judgment.

Reliance on her own judgment was a problem for Nancy Adams, the new marketing manager we met earlier. Nancy's sales team sells electronic control products to various industries. She was intimidated by the lack of structure in her department; what appeared to be freedom and flexibility when she was a sales person looked and felt like a runaway train when she became a new manager. She caught herself stalling her sales team when they pressed her for decisions. Furthermore, she no longer seemed to trust her creativity, so her ideas for sales promotion began to look stale and lifeless. Worse yet, she didn't know what to say when one of her struggling sales persons cautiously ventured an idea for a new product application. Finally, when the performance of her sales persons began to suffer, she forced herself to approach her manager.

Nancy: "I'm really uncomfortable making all these decisions. I'm afraid I'm going to fail—or do something I'm not supposed to do. I'm paralyzed because I'm so worried about doing something wrong."

Nancy's manager: "Your new job requires you to exercise judgment, Nancy. The only mistake you're making is not trusting your judgment. The only situation I want to hear more about is the new product application—and that's only because I care about your sales persons and I want to spread good ideas like that to other parts of the company."

Nancy: "Some manager, huh? I want my people to be bold in the marketplace, but I know I sound timid and full of excuses in the sales meetings."

Nancy's manager: "Every other problem you've mentioned is within your authority and ability to handle. I obviously trust your judgment. So will you, after a few mistakes and a few successes. I wish I could give you a book or a class that would guarantee success every time, but you know that our business changes too fast. This is on-the-job training, Nancy, so get yourself a positive attitude, stop thinking so much about what might go wrong, and just do the best you can. I will support you."

As a manager, Nancy is a "knowledge worker"; her performance depends upon how well she uses her mind (rather than her motor skills). Information, quality, and customer service are her most powerful competitive tools, and these are the tools of the mind. No one can do her thinking for her. As a manager, she is expected to analyze the problem, talk to the appropriate people when necessary, solve the problems, and get the job done.

The manager's job has changed in other ways, too. As a first-line manager, you are likely to be doing the planning and decision making formerly done by middle managers. The rapid pace of change and other competitive pressures have forced most companies to thin the ranks of their middle managers. These leaner organizations can respond more effectively to the changing marketplace. To avoid bureaucracy, they have allowed their managers to become more autonomous.

These new responsibilities require you as a manager to spend more time planning and organizing the work to be done, and less time directly supervising the people who are doing the work. You need new skills to do this; even though you have been successful in the past because of your "hands on" knowledge or because you were a capable administrator, your success as a manager depends on your ability to really *manage* the efforts of others.

The makeup and nature of the work force you supervise has changed dramatically in recent years, too. This requires you to adopt a management style stressing employee collaboration and participation. Workers today are increasingly diverse in background, expectations, and abilities. They are increasingly educated, mindful of the value of their work effort. They are more sophisticated, often placing a high importance on the quality of their work life, their opportunities to develop themselves, and other intangible values such as achievement, prestige, independence, location, enjoyment, and self-realization.

Your employees want to work for a manager who shows respect for them by asking for their input and listening to their ideas. With a shrinking pool of qualified labor, companies cannot afford to remain insensitive to their workers' needs. Today, fewer supervisors see themselves as disciplinarians or distrustful watchdogs for the company because such management styles are no longer effective.

Is your company facing increased competition? Is it struggling to keep up with new customer needs and new technologies? These pressures will continue to affect your job because they force your company to make big changes frequently. If your company cannot react and adopt new technology, for example, sales will soon decline as customers seek better value elsewhere.

In short, the job of the manager changes as the company changes. And why not? The managers are usually the ones leading the process of change (see Figure 2-1).

Figure 2-1
The manager's job has changed.

From		To
Policies and procedures	⟶	High judgment tasks
Activity oriented (doing the right things)	⟶	Results oriented (achieving the right objectives)
Technical skills	⟶	Communication skills
Rigidity and constancy	⟶	Flexibility and responsiveness
Control	⟶	Motivation
Narrow focus	⟶	Broad focus
Internal focus	⟶	Customer focus
Administrative	⟶	Intrapreneurial
Specific responsibilities	⟶	Ambiguity, blurring of roles
Static skills	⟶	Continuous learning

(continued)

Figure 2-1 *(continued)*

Labor/manage-ment conflict	⟶	Labor/manage-ment collabo-ration
Management of white males	⟶	Management of diverse work force
Job security	⟶	Risk, participa-tion, career growth
Disciplinarian	⟶	Coach
People as parts of business	⟶	People as partners in business

YOUR ROLES AS A MANAGER: AN OVERVIEW

If you haven't already done so, obtain a copy of your new job description from your supervisor or the human resources department. You may be told that it is incomplete or out of date, but study it anyway. It will reveal much about the scope of your new job.

Before you became a manager, your job was probably described as a group of activities worded something like this:

"Process this many of those within that much time"
"Deliver . . ."
"Make . . ."
"Test . . ."
"Measure . . ."
"Write . . ."

---

and so on.

Now that you are one of the organization's leaders, the scope of your job is likely to be described in terms of objectives, accountabilities, or outputs relating to the achievement of the organization's goals:

"Raise productivity by three percent . . ."
"Reduce absenteeism by 30 percent . . ."
"Reduce costs by nine percent . . ."
"Develop a scheduling system that allows us to reduce our inventory by 20 percent . . ."

---

and so on. Briefly, the organization is asking you to get something done, and leaving it up to you to decide how to do it, within the rules and values of the organization, of course.

In other words, you are now responsible for improving the performance of those you supervise. What they do and how well they do it are within your control to influence, and therefore you are accountable for it. Their success, or lack of success, depends on you.

How do managers actually manage? Managers manage everything—people, projects, programs, and all the rest—by performing four functions in the following sequence: (1) planning, (2) organizing, (3) influencing, and (4) controlling.

Everything that a manager does relates to one or more of these functions, which together, make up *the management process.*

It hasn't always been so. The management process and the management functions that comprise it were first identified in about 1910 by Henri Fayol, the managing director of a large coal mine in France. He saw the organization as a body—the "body corporate." Fayol viewed the activities of every business organization fitting into six functions: technical (production), commercial (buying, selling, and exchange), financial (finding and employing capital), security (protection of people and property), accounting, and managerial (planning, organization, command, coordination, and control).

All these functions of a business organization were well understood, according to Fayol, except the managerial function, which he believed was mingled with the other functions. Fayol's writings did much to clarify the unique relationships and contributions of the management functions as they relate to the rest of the organization, and he is now generally regarded as the "Father of Modern Management." His five-function process has been modified dozens of times since then to arrive at our current four-function model.

Management is not an activity with a distinct beginning and a definite end. It is an ongoing cycle that repeats itself again and again for everything and everyone whom the manager manages. The sequence in which the functions are performed never varies. Naturally a manager will be at different places in the cycle with each situation, but he or she will always be planning before organizing, influencing before controlling, and so on.

Because the functions of management are meant to improve the organization's productivity, you will find it useful to think about the management process as the *performance improvement process.* Now, management functions are described in terms of skills. This helps us keep in mind what a manager does and why he does it.

The *principles of supervision* are the natural laws of management. These describe how people work together in organizations, and are the focus of Chapter 3.

Communicating about performance is a critical skill because it provides the focus for the other skills. Through communication about performance, all the manager's skills are linked together and directed at the improvement of performance discussed in detail in Chapter 8.

Management is distinct from all the other activities of an enterprise, yet it is not an isolated activity, separate from the other activities of the organization. Rather, it is directly and deeply involved in activities like production, marketing, finance, and every other activity of the company. Management work is not the money-making work of the organization; rather, it maintains the successful operation of all the other activities that do the work of the business.

As discussed in Chapter 1, many managers do not understand the difference between *doing* the work and *managing* the work. Some chairmen, foremen, data processing supervisors, customer service coordinators, group leaders, generals, deans, principals, program directors, medical directors, head nurses, managing editors, sales managers, chief engineers, controllers, partners in accounting firms, and countless others in management jobs are too deeply immersed in the work of their organization. They do not understand that their responsibilities to plan, organize, influence, and control are critical to maintaining the organization and moving it toward its goals.

The management process is a dynamic activity, constantly changing in response to circumstances and opportunities. How much of each of the following management functions you do will be a matter of emphasis for your job.

> *Planning* is the process of determining in advance what should be accomplished and how it should be done. When a manager plans, he or she visualizes the future direction of the work group's effort. A good plan always states an objective and specifies the time and resources needed to accomplish the objective.
>
> For example, the manager of a warehouse crew anticipates the needs to receive and stack new merchandise, load the current orders, and count the inventory. To accomplish these objectives, the manager must plan accordingly. He must have the right tools on hand (forklifts, clipboards, and calculators), schedule enough time to complete the tasks (a day? a week?), and make the necessary adjustments in the work assign-

ments according to how many people are needed.

Organizing is the process of assigning people and allocating resources to accomplish the objectives set in the planning process. This means having qualified people and the resources they need in the right place at the right time so that the organization can succeed. The warehouse manager in the example above must organize a crew of the right size and skill to do the tasks he has planned, and they must have the necessary equipment available when they need it.

When the planned objectives are not met, a manager may decide to reorganize. Are the people who are taking inventory showing up too early, before the current orders have been filled and before the new merchandise has been stocked? The manager has the power to change the organization to find a different combination of workers and resources that will be more productive. He or she may change the work flow, reassign workers to new supervisors, buy new equipment, or physically rearrange the workplace. He or she may change formal relationships, such as having the inventory workers take direction from the stocking foreman, or promote informal relationships, such as having the leaders of the work groups assign ''aisle captains,'' if perceived as helpful to get the work done in a better way.

Influencing is the process of determining or affecting the behavior of others. Managers seek to persuade employees to view their personal objectives as linked to the attainment of the corporate objectives. "What's good for the company is good for all of us" is the message the employees have to understand. Using motivation and leadership, the manager strives to maximize the employee's abilities on behalf of the company. The ability to influence an employee depends on the manager's interpersonal communication skills.

Controlling, the fourth and final management function, means identifying gaps in performance between that which was planned and that which was actually accomplished, and then taking necessary corrective actions. Effective controls provide accurate and timely feedback about performance that can be used to update the organization's plans. Effective controls do more than just identify performance gaps after the fact, however; they also communicate before the employee begins to work just what the expected performance standards are. Effective controls communicate performance expectations early, thereby increasing the likelihood that they will be achieved. "That which is measured is that which is improved" is a popular management maxim.

The planning function does not become credible until there is an organization that can implement the plan. Likewise, good organizing is just theory until the employees are actually motivated to do the work. Influence depends on the control function to keep the work effort channeled. Controls are intertwined with planning. A plan is not complete until it includes good control mechanisms that allow the manager to easily monitor the progress of the plan. Finally, all the functions are integrated by communication skills focused on improving performance.

In the next chapter, we will look at the unwritten rules that guide managers.

3

The Principles of Supervision

Why do organizations continue to function more or less smoothly, in spite of the inevitable conflicts, pressures, and changes to which they are subjected? How can they continue to process and build and ship and sell day after day without breaking down? Are there unwritten rules or concepts that explain the invisible bonds holding organizations together? Yes, there are principles and concepts that serve as the glue to hold organizations together. These are unwritten rules that explain how and why a group of people continue to work together toward a common goal. They are not inviolate, but they do reflect the aspects of human nature that draw us to organizations and keep us working toward the group's success.

DIVISION OF LABOR

The concept of division of labor, also called the specialization of labor, was introduced earlier as a means of determining the functions of an organization. When a manager is organizing a group of people for the first time, it is very useful to think about matching the people to the tasks at hand.

Division of labor principles apply in the operational arena, too. By subdividing all activities into their most basic tasks, managers can be certain of who is responsible for what. They can also write more specific and measurable job descriptions. A foreman on a building maintenance crew, for example, applies the division of labor principle to assign floor polishing, wall painting, duct cleaning, and other jobs. If everyone does his or her own jobs, the building will get cleaned and painted on schedule.

You may see this principle in action first-hand as a "who's doing what" problem. Some of your more experienced workers will know a lot about the jobs of other workers. Perhaps they started in the department as a media planner or oiler or payroll clerk; perhaps they were cross-trained to take over for workers on vacation; or perhaps they just picked it up because they've grown up with the department. These people are obviously very valuable contributors, but what do you do when they want to be involved in everyone else's jobs?

When workers wander far afield from their jobs, confusion and misunderstandings can quickly boil over. You start to hear angry voices saying things like, "Whose job is this, anyway?" and, "Mind your own business!" True, the seasoned pro may be able to do everyone's job better than they can, but he can't do them all.

Watch out for a person who has clearly stopped being a supportive resource to the team and is instead injecting himself into the tasks normally performed by others with the masquerade of "helping" them. You have a powerful cannon loose on your deck. You cannot afford to alienate him, but you have to rein him in or you will be stuck with a meddler who is forever slowing other employees down with suggestions they don't want or need. This person needs to be redirected back to his assignment. If you discover he's bored, give him some real challenges that need his expertise. If he's unable to do his job, and therefore feels compelled to do others' jobs, get him some help. Say to him: "Sure, you can do that job better. You can do lots of other jobs around here, too, and when we ask you for help, we're grateful for your expertise. But your job right now is over here, and we need you to get it done." You must assert the principle of division of labor to prevent confusion in the ranks about who is doing what.

RESPONSIBILITY

Responsibility is an obligation to perform work activities. After we have made a commitment to accept responsibility for a task, our natural inclination is to work to fulfill it. If we accept responsibility, we expect to receive penalties or rewards commensurate with our performance.

Responsibilities are shared in an organization. They are delegated, assumed, avoided, passed on to someone else, and otherwise distributed. The concept of responsibility gives employees their focus; it also enriches their work life with intangible benefits such as self-esteem, job satisfaction, and the respect and praise of their peers. If you assume the responsibility for a company-owned Dairy Queen store, for example, it becomes in a very real sense "your shop": You plan for the grand opening, organize for long-term operations, influence the employees by motivating them and instilling in them the proper attitude about customer service, and control the operations with proper accounting, training, and quality control procedures.

When responsibilities are not clear, the organization suffers because the work does not get done. Ironically, the simplest tasks are often the ones that do not get the attention they need. If a task is not specifically mentioned in a person's job description, it is a potential problem. Nonroutine projects are particularly troublesome because every detail has to be assigned to someone. Everyone who is even remotely involved in a project has the responsibility to help the group by asking, "Who is taking care of this?" Whenever you raise this question, you save yourself from a future headache.

Safety and quality are commonly lost in the category of "everyone's responsibility." Because everyone is responsible, no one is responsible—except someone else! The prudent manager recognizes this and assigns primary responsibility to a quality control specialist or a safety engineer.

The nuclear power plant accident at Three Mile Island, in Pennsylvania in 1979, is an example of how dangerous a situation can be when responsibilities are not clear. Public safety was jeopardized when radioactive gas was released, exposing the citizens in the nearby communities to high levels of radioactivity. A study of the incident revealed that important safety steps had been overlooked and omitted, partially due to confusion about who was responsible for which procedures. Bridge construction, drug formulation, product packaging, automobile manufacturing, and most other businesses have their own versions of this potential problem. The remedy is to acknowledge the confusion and document each operator's responsibility.

AUTHORITY

The companion principle to responsibility is authority, defined as the right to decide, to direct others to take action, and to perform certain duties in the process of achieving organizational goals. It is called a companion principle because responsibility and the authority to take the actions necessary to fulfill the responsibility are usually conferred at the same time. In other words, if a person accepts the responsibility to increase sales 15 percent, for example, he or she will need the authority to hire and fire sales persons, make pricing decisions, target new customers, spend money on product promotion, and perform similar activities. Managers should be mindful that responsibility without authority is doomed to fail.

DELEGATION

The process of assigning responsibility along with the needed authority is called delegation. This is one of the key concepts of management, central to your need to accomplish objectives through the efforts of others.

Figure 3-1
The principles of supervision at work.

Division of Labor	means	"Let's divide the work among us."
Responsibility	means	"I (or you) own this job; you can hold me accountable for it."
Authority	means	"I (or you) get to decide how this is going to get done."
Delegation	means	"You have the responsibility and authority to accomplish this assignment."
Accountability	means	"The buck stops here."
Unity of Command	means	"No matter who else you work with, you are accountable to only one person."

A manager unwilling or unable to delegate is limited to the amount of work he or she is able to do alone. Delegation enables a manager to accomplish more challenging jobs because it extends the manager's capabilities, multiplying the efforts directed toward an objective. Through delegation, a manager can assemble a hand-picked team of persons with specialized talents to focus on a problem.

Delegating does not pass on the ultimate responsibility for the success or failure of an assignment, however. Delegating is an option, another way to get things done, but the final responsibility remains with the manager who made the assignment. You cannot excuse yourself by saying, "It's not my fault. I gave that job to Bob and Julie, and they really messed up." If the wrong person was selected to handle the job, or if the person was not furnished with the required resources, the manager must accept the blame. The manager is likewise entitled to the credit if his decisions to delegate prove to be correct and the work is completed successfully.

The reasons to delegate are numerous, but the most important are listed below:

1. Delegation may result in faster decisions; *upward delegation* to supervisors occurs when subordinates do not trust the supervisors to support decisions made at lower levels. "Kicking it upstairs" for a decision can lead to time-consuming bottlenecks.

2. Delegation may lead to better decisions. The employees closest to the job are usually in an excellent position to solve problems and initiate positive changes.

3. Delegation is a means of developing leadership and other skills in subordinates by giving them opportunities to demonstrate their capabilities.

4. Delegation may improve motivation. When an employee feels he has the trust and confidence of management, he may work harder to justify that trust and live up to heightened expectations.

5. Delegation may also improve the morale of employees. When you trust your employees, you can expect a positive attitude in return. Furthermore, delegation confers a sense of "ownership" of assigned tasks on subordinates, so that they may take more pride in their work.

ACCOUNTABILITY

After an assignment has been delegated and the responsibility and authority have been passed on, the manager is held accountable for the results of his decisions and actions. Accountability is a means of ensuring that the person who is supposed to do a task actually performs it and does it correctly. It is a part of the control function, and becomes important after a task is completed.

Accountability cannot be passed on by the manager. Part of it can be shared with subordinates, but in the end, the highest-level managers are held accountable for the success or failure of the organization.

Yes, the buck really does stop with you!

UNITY OF COMMAND

The unity of command principle is the belief that each person should be accountable to only one supervisor; in other words, each person should have only one boss. This simplifies communication and discipline by eliminating potentially contradictory orders from more than one manager.

Margaret, (manager of the MIS department): "Great idea. But we're something
called a *matrix* organization. I have a lot of
people out on loan to other departments, so
they have two managers: a project manager
who runs the department they are assigned
to and a functional manager—me—at the
same time."

Employee: "Who's really my boss?"

Beyond the confusion over who he or she takes
orders from, the possibility of mischief—playing one
manager against the other—exists. Sometimes, each
manager assumes that the other manager is holding
the employee accountable, when, in fact, neither of
them are.

Margaret: "I solve this problem by teaching my
employee to think of the department manager
as a customer—you know, a real customer,
outside the company, who has certain needs
that we are trying to satisfy. My employee's
assignment then becomes very clear: to meet
the customer's needs.

   Now I think of my people getting in an im-
aginary repair truck every morning and driving out to service the customer, even though
this is all taking place within our building
here. Naturally, I expect to hear from my employees when they have a problem, need advice, or finish the assignment, but the other
manager calls the shots on the job because
he's the customer. We've all got the best in-

terests of the company in common, so among the three of us, we've talked about it enough so that my employee knows who his boss is.''

In the next chapter, we'll examine the first of the four functions of management: planning.

4

Planning Skills

Before a manager does anything, he or she must plan. The manager's plans provide the framework for what happens—and doesn't happen—in the organization. Plans that are practical yield positive results: satisfied customers, high employee morale, and enough profits to fund the company's growth. On the other hand, poor planning leads to late deliveries, rushed schedules that require expensive overtime interspersed with idle machines or workers with nothing to do, inefficient duplication of work, and quarreling and excuse making among the employees.

AN OVERVIEW OF PLANNING

Good plans specify work priorities and how the work is to be done. They answer the twin questions, "What work is really important to do now?" and

"How are we going to get it done?" A plan is ready to be communicated to the people who will implement it only if it states an objective and specifies the time and resources needed to accomplish the objective.

To people being supervised, a manager's role in the planning process may appear to begin and end in his or her department. Actually, every manager makes a contribution to the umbrella corporate planning process by regularly communicating with other members of the management team.

Long-term plans, mid-term plans, and short-term plans fit into a hierarchy of planning that mirrors the management hierarchy. One of the chief advantages of the planning process is the elimination of conflicting plans, cross-purposes between departments, and inefficiency. The plans of each manager must support the overall goals that give the organization its direction.

ADVANTAGES OF PLANNING

"To plan is to predict change."

By planning well, a manager can obtain important advantages for his or her organization. Planning is active, not passive; it causes the planners to shed their "wait and see" attitudes about the future by forcing them to forecast the environment of the future. By imagining what their problems and opportunities will be next month or next year, managers can prepare the organization's best responses. Planning almost always saves time and money.

Planning also gives a company direction in the form of objectives. Based on the "what if" scenarios they forecast, managers know what they can and cannot realistically achieve over a given period of time. Knowing this helps set day-to-day goals and reduces costly shifts in policy and strategy. Another advantage is the sense of teamwork that is fostered when the corporate goals are communicated throughout the company in the form of a plan.

Finally, planning yields valuable insights into the company's problems and opportunities. It is no coincidence that companies that plan are almost always holding favorable positions relative to their competitors. They are able to stay "one step ahead" because they plan.

Planning is no guarantee of success, however. No one can forecast the future and make all the necessary decisions in advance. Precious little in the marketplace is predictable, and even less can be controlled with certainty. In spite of the ambiguities of the future, planning usually helps everyone in the organization function more effectively.

TYPES OF PLANNING

The planning for which management is responsible can be described as long-term planning, mid-term planning, and operational planning. Long-term plans commonly look forward three to five years and beyond. These are called strategic plans because they focus on strategy, and they address the fundamental questions of the company's mission: What is the nature of our business? Are we correct to stay in this business? What long-term trends are likely to affect our customers or ourselves, and how will those

FIGURE 4-1   Rate Your Planning Skills

When I plan, I:

_____ finish on time
_____ write my plan down
_____ refer to my plan and make mid-term corrections
_____ keep my plan in sight
_____ communicate my plan to others
_____ anticipate obstacles
_____ prepare a backup plan
_____ delegate
_____ set deadlines for myself and others
_____ keep track of where my time is spent
_____ keep in mind the value of my time
_____ focus on those activities that will have the greatest impact
_____ review my list of goals
_____ have a clear idea of what I want to accomplish next week
_____ set priorities according to importance, not urgency
_____ concentrate on objectives instead of procedures
_____ isolate myself for quiet thinking time
_____ focus on results, not activities
_____ keep the organization's mission and goals in mind
_____ reward myself for meeting my plan
_____ Total

1 = rarely   2 = occasionally   3 = sometimes
4 = frequently   5 = almost always
When you have added all your points, if your score totals less than 60, you need significant development of your planning skills.

trends affect us? How must we change to maintain or improve our competitive advantage, and what must we do to prepare for those changes?

"Managers are not superhuman, but they are supposed to have a gyroscope on their priorities."

What should this company be doing differently five years from now? How should it be performing financially? How many employees will it have? Strategic plans usually include a mission statement that answers the question, What is our business and what do we ultimately hope to achieve with it? As a new manager, you will have little effect on the strategic plan, but you should know what it is and be able to communicate it to your employees. Ask your manager or human resources department for a copy of it.

Mid-range planning looks forward one to three years and focuses on how to compete in a particular industry or market segment. The mid-range plans are subsets of the long-range plan, addressing many of the same issues within the context of a competitive marketplace. Typical questions asked of a mid-range plan are the following: What changes are going to occur among our customers, suppliers, and competitors, and how must we change to prepare for this new environment? What skills will our personnel need to compete effectively, and what must we do now so that they will be ready? A popular model for this analysis is the S.W.O.T. Analysis developed by the Harvard Business School, which asks managers to list the company's strengths, weaknesses, opportunities, and threats.

FIGURE 4-2 Types of Planning

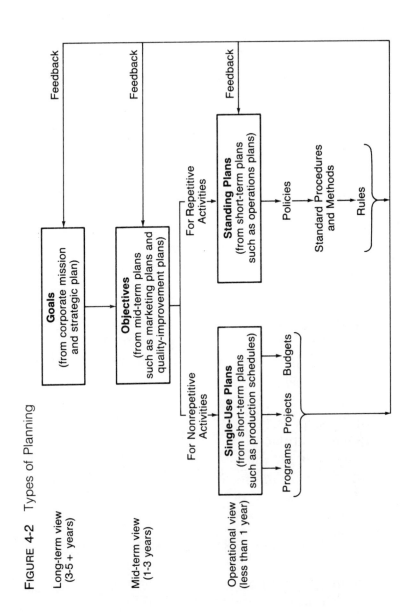

As you would expect, operational or tactical planning focuses on the work that must be done within the next 12 months. These day-to-day, week-to-week plans are concerned with current levels of staffing, the implementation of the marketing plan, vendor reliability, and customer satisfaction, among many other issues. Operational planners ask "how?" and "when?" more often than they ask "What should we be doing next?" and "Why are we doing this?"

The hierarchy of plans is addressed by a hierarchy of managers. Most senior managers do the long-range planning and the lower-level managers supervise the day-to-day operational plans. The most progressive organizations have mechanisms that facilitate frank and dynamic discussion and feedback among the different levels of management. Communication between the people making the plans and the people implementing the plans improves everyone's performance and the overall productivity of the organization.

If plans are for nonrepetitive activities like promotion programs, project development, and budgets, they are further categorized as single-use plans. Repetitive activities governed by policies, standard procedures, and rules are called standing plans.

HOW TO WRITE A GOOD PLAN

Planning is the process of determining in advance what should be accomplished and how it should be done. It is a three-step process:

1. Decide what your priorities are. Define the few large goals that will guide the rest of the planning process, keeping in mind where you are in relation to the goals right now.

2. Develop the midpoint objectives that will support the goals, taking into consideration the barriers and aids that exist in the environment.

3. Divide each objective into simple action plans that will lead to the accomplishment of the objectives and the goals.

Specificity is the key to making a plan successful. A goal, for example, that simply states that a com-

FIGURE 4-3   The Planning Process

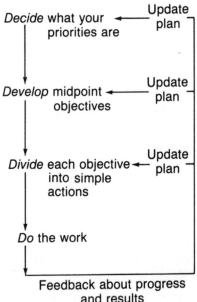

Ask yourself: "What's the most important contribution I can make?"

Decide what your priorities are ← Update plan

Ask yourself: "How will I know I am doing enough of the right work?"

Develop midpoint objectives ← Update plan

Ask yourself: "What short-term action plans will accomplish my objectives?"

Divide each objective into simple actions ← Update plan

Ask yourself: Nothing. What's left to think or talk about? Just do it!

Do the work

Feedback about progress and results

pany wants "to grow" is doomed to remain on the wish list. What kind of growth would satisfy this goal—financial, personnel, market share, number of product categories? Or something not yet mentioned? Without more specific direction, the employees of this company are probably going to grow in different directions. They'll be busy all right, but they probably won't be doing the same things or the right things. At best, they will stay out of each other's way; more likely, they will get into conflict because the company cannot grow in all ways simultaneously with limited resources.

On the other hand, think about an objective or goal that says nothing more than "to improve the company's productivity." What does this mean? Does it mean cut back to reduce expenses, or does it mean expand the business with the 25 most profitable accounts? Perhaps it means neither, but no one will know until it is too late, after time and money are misspent. We'll discuss how to write good objectives later in this chapter.

CHARACTERISTICS OF GOOD PLANNING

Successful plans are specific, but they are also flexible. Many managers have a "best case" plan that is used if and when a situation unfolds as expected. He or she also has a "worst case" plan to fall back on when the original plan is upset by surprise circumstances. Between the best case and the worst case plans lies the "target plan," which will probably reflect the actual situation. The prudent manager watches carefully for signs of how well the target plan is working, and then adjusts accordingly, perhaps by hiring a new advertising agency, increasing production, or cancelling orders for raw materials.

Good planning reflects reality. The objective-writing exercise is a formal way of asking whether this result is really attainable. If the success of a delivery service hinges on getting the average order delivered within 35 minutes of the customer's phone call, and the drivers' best average has been 42 minutes, the objective may be unrealistic. Simply wanting a change to occur is not enough to make it happen.

"Successful managers plan to plan, and then do it."

Plans should also reflect the skills, knowledge, and attitudes of the people implementing them. In the case noted above, perhaps the delivery persons were unfamiliar with the streets of the city and routinely had to consult their maps. If that is their level of skill and knowledge, the manager of the delivery service must take this into consideration. If they have never performed the desired activity successfully at the standard set by the objective, they cannot be expected to do so without changes that make the new performance possible. Do they need some kind of training? Do they need two-way radios or car telephones in their vehicles? Should they be strategically located in advance throughout the city? Can they improve their response time if assigned to smaller geographic areas? If the manager is committed to the new performance objective, he must come up with a workable plan that will make the change happen.

Good plans should state specific ways to achieve the desired results. In the case of the delivery service just mentioned, the manager may plan on meeting the target of 35 minutes by reorganizing the route map, putting telephones in all the cars, and providing additional training to the drivers. If an objective is supported by reasonable and specific actions like these that make the objective possible to achieve, the objective should be given a chance to succeed.

Finally, plans have to be communicated upward and downward in the organization's hierarchy. The delivery drivers cannot be held accountable for new levels of performance if the plans were not communicated to them. Also, the manager may not expect the support of senior management when asked for more money to buy the telephones if they do not understand or accept the plan.

HOW TO WRITE GOOD OBJECTIVES

One of the truisms among mangers is, "Good direction yields good results." If managers expect to obtain optimal results through the efforts of their employees, they must make the extra effort to communicate their precise expectations to those employees.

Objectives and goals, used here synonymously, are clearly the mechanisms that link a plan to the actions that make it a reality. The process of writing down objectives forces people to think through the steps they'll have to take in order to accomplish the objective. This is more than mental exercise; by breaking down the large tasks required into simple actions, the difficulty of the tasks is diminished.

The responsibility of the manager is to establish *goals, objectives,* and *action plans* with the following seven characteristics:

a. They should state the purpose of this objective ("In order to increase productivity by 10 percent, . . .").

b. They should be measurable ("assemble 50 additional television sets . . .").

c. They should specify a time frame within which these goals will be achieved (". . . every eight-hour shift . . .").

d. They should specify the resources needed ("by operating an additional assembly line for subassemblies . . .").

e. They should specify the quality of the output ("without increasing the rate of rejects above two percent").

f. They should be challenging, but attainable.

g. They should be expressed in writing to increase commitment and understanding while reducing confusion.

The more specific an objective is, the more likely it is to be accomplished. By quantifying how much

Figure 4-4
Objective-Setting Worksheet

What's the action? (verb)	What's the result? (noun)	When's it due? (time frame)	Who will check? (monitor)	What's the purpose? (reason/purpose)

For each objective, how will you know you're making progress?

Indicators | When's it due?
(activity) | (time frame)

will be done, when it will be finished, and who will do it using which resources, the plan leaves less possibility of misunderstanding or error. Figure 4-4 suggests a format for writing clear, workable objectives.

HOW TO WRITE GOOD ACTION PLANS

If the objectives are precisely stated and quantified, they will provide clear direction to the people actually doing the work. Clear objectives lead to clear work plans, also called *activity plans* or *action plans.* Objectives state what must be done; action plans expand on the details of the activities to explain how it will be done. An objective is typically no longer than a paragraph, but an action plan can be many pages in length. An action plan can be thought of as a plan within a plan that specifies all the work details that must be identified, assigned, and accomplished.

The best way to write an action plan is to imagine doing the work, step-by-step, and then write down the key details. The following 10-point checklist describes the action planning process for a moderately complex project:

1. List everything that must be done to accomplish the objective.

2. List the tasks to be done in the order they should be finished.

3. Identify by name the person(s) who will be doing which tasks.

4. List the resources necessary for the completion of each task.

5. Note the time needed for each task, including the estimated delivery time needed for materials not already on hand.

6. Consider the constraints that might upset this plan, and note the steps that can be taken to avoid them.

7. Write the plan on a chart that reflects the passage of time such as an event calendar or a Gantt chart.

8. Identify the control points that will mark the progress of activity. (For a complete discussion, see Chapter 7.)

9. Develop a backup plan just in case you cannot accomplish the objective or finish the action plan, or are only partially successful.

10. Update the plan periodically to reflect feedback and the most current data.

Plans that are successful, regardless of their level in the hierarchy, specify what or how much should be accomplished and when the work will be done. A plan is ready to be communicated to those who will implement it only when clear, measurable objectives are supported by well-reasoned action plans.

In the next section, we will look at how the planning process is applied.

MANAGEMENT BY OBJECTIVES

Objectives have proven to be very useful in the measurement and control of planning and performance. In fact, the practice of directing an organization with objectives has matured during the past two decades into a formal management style called management by objective (MBO).

Management by objectives is a process in which supervisors and subordinates identify common goals, agree on objectives that specify how the subordinate will contribute to the accomplishment of the goals, and agree to use the measured results as a guide for evaluating the subordinate's performance. The structure and guidelines of the MBO approach forces managers to communicate with each other about difficult subjects that might otherwise be left to chance. It also forces managers to plan explicitly instead of simply responding to opportunities and crises as they arise.

MBO is a more systematic and rational approach to management than *crisis management, fire fighting,* or *seat-of-the-pants* methods. It is also different from reactive or reflexive management approaches because it focuses on achieving measurable results. Philosophically, it is result oriented, and it uses mutually agreed-on objectives as the primary basis of motivation, evaluation, and control efforts.

Here is how an MBO program works: Imagine you are the manager of the data processing (DP) department. You must meet with your employees to discuss the department's goals, which in this case are changing because of the number of microcomputers being purchased for use throughout the company,

FIGURE 4-5   The Management by Objective (MBO) Process

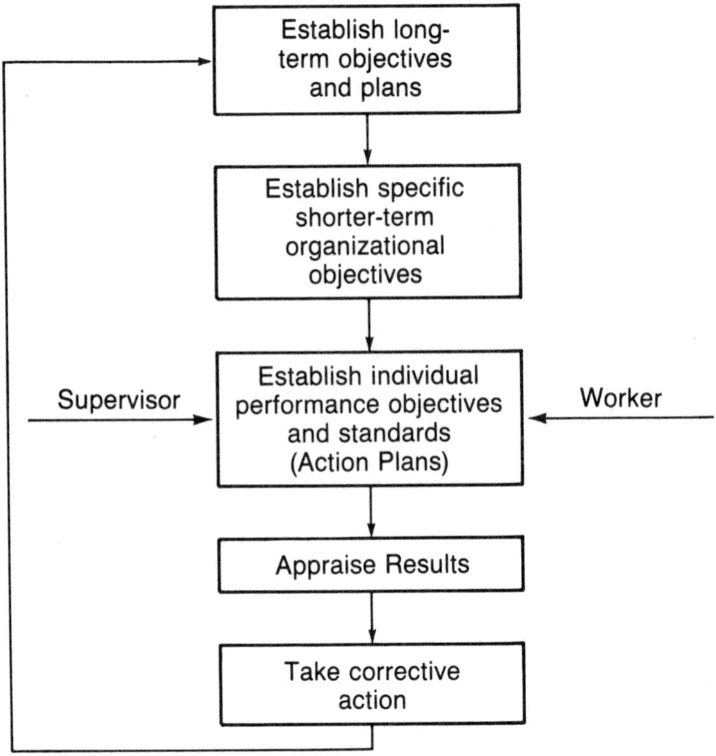

```
        ┌──────────────────────┐
   ┌───▶│   Establish long-    │
   │    │   term objectives    │
   │    │      and plans       │
   │    └──────────┬───────────┘
   │               │
   │    ┌──────────▼───────────┐
   │    │  Establish specific  │
   │    │     shorter-term     │
   │    │    organizational    │
   │    │      objectives      │
   │    └──────────┬───────────┘
   │               │
   │    ┌──────────▼───────────┐
Supervisor ─▶│ Establish individual │◀─ Worker
   │    │ performance objectives│
   │    │    and standards     │
   │    │    (Action Plans)    │
   │    └──────────┬───────────┘
   │               │
   │    ┌──────────▼───────────┐
   │    │   Appraise Results   │
   │    └──────────┬───────────┘
   │               │
   │    ┌──────────▼───────────┐
   │    │   Take corrective    │
   │    │       action         │
   │    └──────────┬───────────┘
   └───────────────┘
```

including your department. It is reasonable to assume that the role of the DP department will change because many of the routine reports will soon be generated without involvement from your DP staff. In essence, your department is becoming less of a batch-processing operation and more of a microcomputer support resource. Communicating the new goals of the department to your employees will probably require several lengthy discussions.

Next, you and your employees suggest objectives that support the attainment of the agreed-upon goals.

In this case, completely new objectives must be written to help the department fulfill its new role as a support resource for microcomputer users. The current objectives that relate to batch-processing assignments probably need to be updated. What else? Are any new programs needed? Together, you and your employees establish (a) what the employees will do, (b) how soon the work will be done, (c) what resources or approaches will be used, and (d) how the employees' performances will be measured. You also agree on the next date to meet so the plan can be evaluated.

"Writing a plan is easier than reading it a month later."

The strongest advantage of the MBO process is the access to the decision-making process that it provides for employees who are low on the corporate ladder. This has two distinct benefits. First, it gives each employee some control over his or her work plan. This heightens the employee's commitment to the objectives and enhances the likelihood that the objectives will be accomplished. Second, the company receives the benefits of the employee's input, which may include the most accurate descriptions of situations that relate to the objectives and new suggestions for improving productivity for the management. Of course, the MBO process can also result in a higher morale among the work force.

The MBO process begins with strong support and commitment from upper management. MBO depends on enthusiastic participation by employees at all levels of the company; after all, they are the ones who make the extra effort to communicate and make the process work. If senior management does not genuinely trust the subordinates or believe the MBO process is worth the commitment, the wrong attitude will be communicated and will cripple the process.

You will notice that the MBO process does for the individual what the planning process does for the company. The MBO action plans translate the corporate goals and objectives into performance objectives and standards for individuals. Just like in the company-wide planning process, specificity as to what is to be done and when it is to be completed is crucial.

Critics of the MBO approach caution that some employees are not ready to participate in the building of their own action plans. There is a tendency on the part of some people to overcommit to what they can do. They are anxious to please and sincerely believe in their optimistic forecast when they make plans, but they may be unrealistic. For example, if a production engineer commits to doubling the number of drawings he will complete in the next three months and no substantive changes have been made in his other assignments to make this possible, he has set himself up to fail. This engineer's manager should counsel him to think more about how the higher output will be attained, and then help him set a more realistic figure. If this coaching and counseling does not occur in an atmosphere that promotes trust, the employee will lose confidence in the process and stop actively participating.

"People have to learn they live and die by their plans, their record of choices. If there is no accountability, the plan becomes a fiction. If no one actually means to do this stuff, anything goes to make the plan look good."

Critics of the MBO process have also voiced concern about the difficulty of setting meaningful goals, about excessive paperwork, about excessive requirements to maintain the system, and about a tendency in some companies to focus too much on the short-term plans at the expense of the long-term plans.

Nevertheless, the general consensus is that MBO is an excellent model for planning and controlling. Many employees and managers may not need a formal planning system all the time, but most find the MBO principles of specificity, measurement, and written action plans an excellent way to avoid misunderstandings and inefficiencies.

Furthermore, the MBO approach is also generally acknowledged as one of the best tools for controlling the results of the company's plans. The objectives force managers and their workers to communicate their expectations for performance, so that monitoring performance becomes much more straightforward. The workers should be able to know just how well they are doing at any time, without involving the manager, thereby empowering them with more self-management. This is a move away from subjective performance evaluations, and it is generally regarded as a more equitable and quicker way to identify performance problems.

WHY PLANS FAIL

1. *They are unrealistic.* If expectations are unrealistic to begin with, the plan is doomed. Because we naturally want to please the people who are important to us, especially our boss, we may develop a tendency to agree too quickly to perform impossible tasks. Assuring a co-worker you can do something only because you know that he wants to hear "just the good news" compounds your error in judgment: Not only will you fail to deliver as promised, but you will be labeled as an unreliable performer who cannot plan well. To keep expectations realistic, strive to gather enough of the critical data to go forward with confidence.

2. *They do not take the team into account.* How many of us have fantasized a plan involving our team members—without seeking their input? It's common sense: If we want someone to join our plan, we have to make sure that
   a. The person is willing to participate and will do a fair share,
   b. The person is able and has the skills and time,
   c. The person does not have conflict with other priorities. (Who will choose which of the priorities get attention?)

3. *They lack meaningful checkpoints.* Nearly as failure-prone are plans that postpone making the tough go/no go decisions.

"If a manager does not believe a plan will succeed, it will fail."

4. *They fail to provide performance feedback.* Plans must specify desired outcomes in measurable terms; then, the persons involved in the plans must frequently and frankly communicate about their progress.

SUMMARY

Planning is not a free-standing activity, independent of the other functions of management. Nor is planning to be performed as an afterthought following a scheduling crisis or a disappointing performance. Planning is the framework within which all work occurs. Planning sets the standards against which performance will be measured and ultimately improved.

To manage means to achieve the organization's objectives through the efforts of others. When those efforts are evaluated in relation to a plan, performance gaps are evident.

Planning begins a continuous loop of performance guidance and performance feedback. Performance guidance is the form of plans, and performance standards are in the form of measurable objectives; the feedback is in the form of evaluation and corrective action. The manager decides what to do about the performance problem, including changing the plan to reflect more realistic expectations.

The management by objective (MBO) approach to planning is a useful model that stresses specificity, quantitative measurement, and regular two-way communication between managers and their employees.

In the following chapter, we will discuss the next function of management: Organizing.

"The amount of work expands to fill the time allotted to complete it." Parkinson's Law

---

5

Organizing Skills

AN OVERVIEW OF ORGANIZING

Organizing is the process of assigning people and allocating resources to accomplish the objectives set in the planning process. This means having qualified people and the resources they need in the right place at the right time so that the action plan can succeed. During the planning process you decided *what* you are going to do; organizing is establishing *how* to do it.

Organizing is an ongoing concern. When planned objectives are not met, a manager may decide to reorganize. If the people taking inventory are showing up too early, before the current orders have been filled and before the new merchandise has been stocked, the manager has the power to change the organization to find a different combination of people and resources that will be more productive. He may change the work flow, reassign workers to new supervisors, buy new equipment, or physically rearrange the workplace. He may change formal relationships, such as having the inventory people take direction from the stocking foreman, or promote informal reationships, such as having the leaders of the work groups assign "aisle captains," if he thinks it will help get the work done in a better way. Organizing is figuring out how to make the action plan happen within the company's formal and informal organizations.

UNDERSTANDING YOUR FORMAL ORGANIZATION

Take a blank piece of paper and write ME with a box around it in the center of the paper. List below this box everyone who reports directly to you and draw a line to them. Off to the side, list the people you interact with and draw solid lines or dotted lines to them. Finally draw boxes above you to represent as much of the rest of the organization as you know. This is a thumbnail sketch of your formal organization.

The formal organization prescribes formal relationships among people and resources in order to accomplish goals. It is important for you to know how your company is organized; it is just as important for you to understand *why* it's organized the way it is.

The dominant strategy of a company leads to its structure. A company creates a formal organization to maximize its human and other resources, and this

Figure 5-1

An Organization's Strategy to Reach Its Objectives Dictates Its Organizational Structure

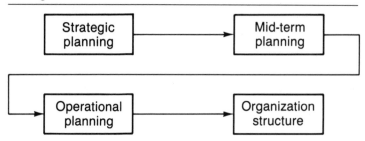

formal organization depends in large part on what the company wants to accomplish.

The typical formal organization has a system of reporting, responsibility, and authority that reflects the formal power of the organization members. An informal system of interpersonal relationships, called the *informal organization,* springs up around the formal organization. For a company to work at its maximum effectiveness, the formal and informal organizations have to be supportive of each other.

You can be sure that your company's formal organization is generally suited to meet the needs of your business. Like most companies, yours probably evolved through different phases as it matured. Your company is organized—and reorganized—after periodic evaluations of the objectives of the business. The accomplishment of the company's objectives is the only good reason to organize in the first place, and it remains the only good reason to reorganize.

If a company is in a highly competitive industry like consumer electronics, for example, its organizational structure must provide certain types of communication and service at the point of sale. This type of company needs to be supported by a decentralized network of loyal and service-oriented retail dealers. The Federal Bureau of Investigation, on the other hand, has different organizational objectives that lead to a highly centralized system of information processing and autonomous field agents.

With its objectives in mind, the company must next decide what types of functions or work must be performed to accomplish those objectives. A manufacturer can organize around the major functions of production and marketing, for example.

Some functions are naturally associated with other functions, such as production with shipping, accounting with bookkeeping, engineering with research, production with quality control, and sales with marketing. If these functions can be grouped together, it is likely that the organization will operate more efficiently because people who have to speak with each other frequently will be in close proximity. How functions are grouped depends on the relative importance of the functions in a particular company. The process of grouping related functions or major work activities into manageable units is known as *departmentalization.*

Occasionally, you may be frustrated with the apparent illogical nature of your company's formal organization, but you can be confident that it is set up so that it can meet certain needs. The needs it is meeting may not be 100% current, which means the formal organization is lagging behind the company's development instead of leading it, but you are better off accepting it the way it is. Work within the structure you have for now. Your energies are better spent on concerns in which you can have a near-term positive impact.

When businesses develop their optimal organization, they usually find that parts of the company are centralized and other parts are decentralized. A computer manufacturer, for example, may have a centralized manufacturing facility, but a decentralized network of service providers spread throughout the country. Again, the structure is a reflection of the organization's objectives.

Decentralization describes a physical relationship, but it also describes a management style. The degree of decentralization in a company can be quickly ascertained by asking one question: Which decisions are made by whom? If the local managers are allowed to make decisions involving large sums of money or affecting many employees, the organization is highly decentralized. On the other hand, if even the senior managers must "check with headquarters" to get approval on routine matters, the organization is highly centralized.

Regardless of the level of centralization a company selects, each position has either a line or a staff relationship with the other positions. Line departments are directly involved in accomplishing the primary purpose of the organization. These are the core functions, processes, or departments that the company is organized around, such as the production department, the smelting division, or the marketing group.

Staff departments provide line departments with advice and assistance in specialized areas like personnel, finance, and research. The staff managers support the line managers and line workers at every level in the organization. The successful organization develops staff departments only to the size required to adequately service the needs of the line departments. Staff positions are auxiliary, described as either (a) advisory, such as the legal department; (b) service, such as the research department, personnel department, and maintenance department; or (c) control, such as the accounting department or quality control department.

Realizing that the formal organization exists as it does for a reason may make it easier for you to work with it. The formal organization has been thoughtfully established to maximize the effective deployment of the company's resources, and you can use the formal organization to your advantage to accomplish your goals. Ask your supervisor for a copy of the company's organizational chart. If no copies are available, gather information and piece one together yourself. At the very least, this will help you know with whom you should speak when you want to get something done.

UNDERSTANDING YOUR INFORMAL ORGANIZATION

Did you ever wonder why some persons in your company always seem to get things done with less effort than others? Did you ever wonder why some decisions languish in red tape and procedures, whereas other decisions are made quickly and efficiently? You are watching the informal organization in action.

The informal organization surrounds the formal organization. It is a complex and dynamic network of interpersonal relationships among organization members. These relationships cannot be diagrammed as can the formal organization, yet they are just as important to the smooth operation of any group of people. By their nature, they are different for every company and are continually changing.

A company depends on its formal organization to provide a stable framework for starting and finishing work assignments. In the practical world, however, the members of the formal organization also modify the organization's structure to meet their own needs in carrying out the action plan, thereby creating an informal organization within and alongside the formal organization. Ideally, these organizations are mutually supportive and reinforce each other; when they are in conflict, the effectiveness of the company is crippled.

The informal organization is evident throughout the company in the form of informal or ad hoc work groups and friendships that cross functional lines. Customers may not be able to describe a company's informal organization, but they know it exists when they benefit from its spirit of cooperation and service. The informal organization has been described as the "human" side of the formal organization, and it is the intangible "personality" or "corporate culture" that distinguishes one enterprise from another.

The informal organization can never be completely controlled. Even if it were possible to do so, it might not be desirable. In this section, we'll examine how you can work with the informal organization, why it exists, and its benefits and costs. In the process, you will gain a deeper understanding of organizational power and politics.

MAKING USE OF THE INFORMAL ORGANIZATION

Managers have mixed feelings about the informal organization, recognizing that it is very influential and yet generally beyond their control. The informal organization can add much to the quality of work life and overall productivity, but it also has the potential to sabotage the plans of managers.

Acknowledging the existence of the informal organization is the manager's first step toward understanding it. It is an inevitable, auxiliary structure that grows naturally out of human social processes. The manager cannot control it precisely, but he or she can create an environment that nurtures the informal organization in such a way that it contributes significantly to the realization of the organization's formal objectives.

A successful manager can attract the support of the informal organization. If the manager understands the informal network of power holders, he or she can focus his efforts on gaining the adjustments and accommodations he wants from these people. This conscious, directed use of the manager's power is commonly referred to as *organizational politics,* which is defined as interpersonal interactions that establish, acquire, transfer, and exercise power. The notion of politics carries an unfairly negative connotation. To the extent that we all want to be effective and gain the cooperation of those around us, we all need to participate in politics to some degree.

Finally, managing the informal organization requires an appreciation of its nature and its benefits.

The manager must learn to live with the informal organization's vagueness ("Who started that rumor?"), its spirit ("You people surprise me with your attitude."), and the strength of its power ("In spite of everything I've tried, the team members persist in following the lead of someone else."). Like it or not, managers are a part of the informal organization by virtue of being members of the business. Successful managers learn how to use their personal power to become active and effective participants in the informal organization.

WHY DOES THE INFORMAL ORGANIZATION EXIST?

The informal organization is an inevitable by-product of social interactions among people. To eliminate an informal organization would mean changing human nature or reducing the size of the organization to one person! In addition, there are at least three specific influences that support the continuation and regeneration of informal organizations.

First, the informal organization is a source of satisfaction for its members. We are a socially oriented society, and we want and need the companionship of peers. We are happiest when we are working among friends, and most of us value the sense that we "belong" to a network of friends at work. Surveys of worker attitudes reveal that one of the chief reasons for remaining with an employer, in spite of unsatisfactory conditions or low advancement potential, is "because of the friends at work."

Second, the informal organization is a source of support for its members. The informal network helps its members solve problems, learn the organization's unwritten rules, overcome obstacles to success through personal coaching, sympathize with individual and group difficulties, and generally keep each other out of trouble. A person who cannot gain the support of his or her peer group is often unable to be effective.

Finally, the informal organization exists because it is a source of information for its members. Information is power in any organization, and most formal communication systems are inadequate in providing the news that is most important or interesting to employees. Memos, newsletters, and bulletin board postings are helpful, but they cannot compare with the company "grapevine" for the latest gossip and behind-the-scenes reporting. Employees depend on the informal organization for timely information about the positive and negative events in the company so that they can prepare themselves for the results.

The informal communication channels provide more than just news; they are also important conduits for sharing experiences, fostering innovation and cooperation, generating support for new ideas, expressing consensus, collecting data for planning purposes, and directly or indirectly influencing people, groups, and events.

STRUCTURE OF THE INFORMAL ORGANIZATION

The informal organizaion is not without structure. Like the formal organization, the informal organization is based on the relative power an individual holds, but it encompasses a broader base of personal power in addition to the power associated with a formal position of authority.

Power is a complex concept, but for our purposes, we can define it simply as the ability of one person to influence the behavior of another. Power is neither good nor bad, but simply an inevitable aspect of every human association, formal or informal. The power structure of a company's informal organization, which essentially links people together on an interpersonal level, is too complex to depict with a two-dimensional organizational chart. How the informal organization works, however, can be understood by examining the different types of personal power.

There are five types of personal power, most of which are not under the control of management.

Positional Power When a person is in a position of formal authority, he or she has legitimate

Figure 5-2
Types of Personal Power

Positional	"Do this because I'm the boss."
Reward	"Do this and I will make it worth your effort."
Referent	"Do as I do."
Coercive	"Do this or else."
Expert	"Do this because I know what to do and you don't."

power. Group members believe a person with formal authority ought to have influence over them because of the unique responsibilities associated with the formal position. Most people believe it is their duty to obey a policeman or a vice president because of the formal authority these two positions carry, even though most people are not directly accountable to these positions. Because of their positions, it is assumed that those with formal authority "know what is right."

Reward Power   Reward power is derived from a person's ability to reward another person. Some reward powers are formal, such as when a manager rewards a person with a promotion or an increase in compensation. Informal reward powers are exercised by co-workers and informal leaders in the form of acceptance or rejection by co-workers, recognition for performance, certain types of assistance, or the sharing or withholding of information.

Referent Power   This form of power is evident when group members identify with the power holder. If they like the power holder and want to be like him, they will do what the power holder asks out of a sense of respect, liking, and desire to be liked in return. President John F. Kennedy had strong referent power; his admonition, "Ask not what your country can do for you, but what you can do for your country," became a rallying cry for a generation of Americans committed to social action through organizations like the Peace Corps.

Coercive Power Coercive power is the power to punish or remove rewards. In the informal organization, this can take the form of avoidance, withdrawal of friendship, or excluding a person from group activities or discussion. When exercised by several group members at once, this type of punishment by peers can be very powerful. No one likes to be punished; therefore, use of this type of power can be counterproductive in the long run.

Expert Power This very effective form of power is based on a person's special knowledge or skill. When other group members recognize a person's unique ability to contribute to their collective success, they naturally defer to him or her.

Experts can be troublesome to manage. If a computer programmer, for example, becomes so knowledgeable about a computer system that he or she is indispensable, the manager with the formal authority may be reluctant to discipline him or her for fear that the programmer will quit or sabotage the system. This highlights the inherent conflict between line and staff positions: The line position has the formal authority and legitimate power, whereas the staff positions depend on informal, expert power. The line manager may have the authority to manage, but in practice, his power is shared among the experts in the informal organization. Imagine what happens at a staff meeting when the line manager says, ''We're going to handle that problem by doing such and such,'' and one or more experts in the group says, ''That's wrong, it's a bad idea.'' The most successful line managers have at least one area of expertise, and are prudent enough to ask for the advice of the experts in other matters.

BENEFITS OF THE INFORMAL ORGANIZATION

After managers accept the inevitability of the informal organization, they can begin to focus on its benefits and strive to create the environment to foster its significant contributions. The chief benefits are:

To help communication.   The grapevine is the informal communication network that coexists with the formal or official channels of communication. The informal organization can transmit information throughout a company faster than the official channels with a degree of accuracy that can be astonishing. Informal communications can be highly selective and very responsive, too. The official channels of communication, such as memos, meetings, newsletters, and others, are still needed to provide complete and credible information, but the grapevine is a valuable contribution of the informal organization.

To help get tasks accomplished.   Managers do not always acknowledge when they use the informal organization, but they invariably rely upon it to get work done. When subordinates are granted the flexibility to cross the "official" lines of the formal organization chart in order to solve problems, they are using the informal organization. Imagine how ponderous and inefficient an organization would be if all requests for action and information had to be channeled through one or more supervisors! The informal organization provides an effective framework for problem solving that makes good use of the subordinates' interpersonal skills and capitalizes on their natural desire to do their job well.

To increase worker satisfaction.   Because of the informal organization, employees are more satisfied with their jobs. They are more confident that their contributions are recognized and appreciated, they are more secure about their jobs because they know what is going on in the company, and they are more committed and loyal because they care about their relationships with their co-workers. These intangible features of the informal organization translate into tangible benefits for the organization, such as lower turnover rates, lower recruitment expenses, less absenteeism, a better safety record, and even higher job performance. The informal organization is the extension of our natural desire to build satisfying relationships with our co-workers.

To complement the formal organization.   The informal organization augments the formal organization in several important ways. First, it provides temporary assistance to those who need on-the-job training. Almost everyone needs to talk through a problem or situation at some time, and there are no boxes for informal advisors or mentors on the formal organization chart. Without an informal support network, people would be trying to perform without feedback or advice, isolated and alienated.

Also, managers find that they can supervise more people when they have the support of an active informal organization. By trusting subordinates to interact with each other regularly, a manager needs to spend less time "micromanaging" every action of every employee. Managers who are genuinely interested in achieving the organization's objectives through the efforts of others will not pass up the opportunity to use the resources and power of the informal organization.

Finally, the informal organization complements the formal organization by challenging and encouraging better management. An informal organization that draws out the best efforts from subordinates will draw out the best efforts from the managers, too. Managers should realize that worker cooperation and enthusiasm affect the organization's performance; not wanting to lose this positive momentum generated by the informal organization, the manager will work hard to make the most of his or her opportunities. If the manager and subordinates are mutually supportive, yet challenging each other to be the best they can be, they both benefit from a more successful organization.

COSTS OF THE INFORMAL ORGANIZATION

The informal organization is not without shortcomings. Because it cannot be controlled, it can disrupt routines, undermine management's directives, depress morale, sabotage operations, and discourage innovation.

Operationally, the informal organization can make or break a company. If the leaders of the informal organization decide to rebel or thwart the wishes of management, the formal organization can do very little before it happens. With sufficient peer pressure, the informal organization's leadership may be able to slow down and otherwise disrupt the efficient operation of the business by persuading the other employees to stop doing their jobs as well as they can. Fortunately, most people realize that permanently crippling the company will hurt each employee in the long run. Widespread and malicious actions rarely continue for very long, giving way to discussions and negotiations among the factions that disagree. This is the negative effect of the informal organization using its power, but it can have a positive outcome if communication within the organization improves.

A more insidious cost of the informal organization is lowered productivity caused by role conflict, conformity, and a resistance to change. The personal influence an informal leader has with an employee may conflict with formal management. The resulting confusion will almost certainly slow down the work of the employee. At best, the employee will struggle to satisfy the wishes of two bosses; at worst, he will be forced to sacrifice his work record in the tug-of-war between the manager and the informal leader.

The "group think" promoted by the informal organization can lead to a numbing conformity. In organizations with strong informal networks, individual differences, personal expression, and personal ambition may be discouraged. "We don't do things like that here" and "You're making the rest of us look bad" and "You have to try harder to fit in" are some of the comments a worker might hear from the informal leaders. Petty jealousies and competition may also result in a common level of mediocre performance.

For the same reasons, new ideas and innovation are not always welcome. "We've always done it this way—if it isn't broken, don't fix it" is a typical remark indicating a reluctance to try new ideas. This attitude can stop new ideas before they have a chance to work.

Managers must ultimately accept the reality of the existence of the informal organization and recognize that additional time and effort must be invested to gain its support and cooperation. To ignore the informal organization is to ignore the basic nature of organizations and the manner in which people work together.

SUMMARY

Successful organizations do not just happen; they are carefully and thoughtfully organized to accomplish their most important objectives. This usually means that they are organized around their dominant functions or work activities, such as marketing, production, and accounting. Then, the basic functions are joined with related but subordinate subfunctions to create departments. The resulting relationships make up the formal organization and can be diagrammed on an organizational chart.

The formal organization and the individual worker are mutually dependent upon each other, and as they join together, they change each other and create an informal organization. The informal organization is a complex and dynamic network of interpersonal relationships between organization members. This difficult-to-describe and uncontrollable informal organization can make an enormous difference in the success of the formal organization.

Ideally, the informal organization is supportive of the formal power structure. At its worst, the informal organization can subvert and dilute the efforts of the formal management. In any case, the informal organization must be acknowledged as an inherent aspect of every group of employees. The prudent manager learns to use sources of personal power, such as referent and expert power, to gain the cooperation of the informal organization. The manager's success can be measured by the success of the organization.

You may occasionally experience frustration and a sense of powerlessness within your organization. You can mediate these feelings by exercising your managerial authority to make organizational changes within your department and your work groups. In fact, you probably have considerable power to influence the results of your group by taking advantage of your formal and informal organization.

6

Influencing Skills

Business folklore is rich with stories about companies achieving extraordinary success with ordinary employees. When asked how theirs became such high performance organizations, the firms' presidents modestly say, "We're lucky. We have good people."

In fact, luck has little to do with good performance on the job. More likely, the companies have good managers who can motivate and lead others. By directing the efforts of others, these managers see to it that their organizations' objectives are accomplished. This activity is the third function of management: influencing.

THE MANAGER IS AN INFLUENCER

The manager is responsible for making the organization get things done. As we learned in earlier chapters, he or she begins by planning what the organization is going to do, then, organizes the resources required to get the work done. After planning and organizing, the manager is logically the person best prepared to supervise the implementation of the plans—IF he can persuade others to help him.

Inevitably, managing means completing tasks through the efforts of other persons. Assembling lamps, promoting a new product, erecting a building—no matter what the task, the manager cannot succeed alone. To see the plans implemented, the manager must influence the actions or behaviors of others and direct their efforts. The manager's success is inherently tied to the successful completion of tasks performed by others. Some managers are successful at their jobs; others are not.

Managers influence people by motivating them and leading them. Motivation and leading are interpersonal skills that communicate the relationship between an employee's needs and the organization's objectives. By motivating and leading, the manager can build a task-oriented team, a cohesive and efficient work unit, thereby amplifying the productivity of the group.

Motivation is defined as the willingness to put forth effort in the pursuit of organizational goals. It is a level of activity, a behavior that can be observed. Motivation is not the same as job performance: A person can be highly motivated to program computers and still be evaluated as incompetent. Motivation is as complex as human nature, and one person's reasons for working are likely to be slightly different from those of someone else. Nevertheless, if a manager has a basic understanding of motivation theory, he or she will be better prepared to influence employee efforts and thereby improve performance.

Leadership is that combination of personal characteristics that earn a person the privilege of influencing a group more than anyone else. Not all leaders are managers, but every manager must lead in order to be effective. Leadership is the role performed by the person who speaks up and persuasively communicates the organizational objectives, thus energizing the motivation process.

Understanding motivation helps the manager to know WHAT to say; understanding leadership helps him know HOW to say it. There is no best way to motivate or lead people; however, there are basic guidelines and principles, and these will be the focus of this chapter.

GETTING RESULTS THROUGH MOTIVATION

The challenge of all managers is to effectively motivate their workers to work toward the organization's objectives. The more we understand about motivation, the more likely we will be able to effectively influence or direct the behavior of employees. Thanks to much study by social scientists, contemporary management recognizes that motivation is a complicated process. The important aspects to keep in mind when discussing motivation are the following:

- Motivation is a set of psychological processes that energize voluntary behavior. Most motivation theories suggest that the psychological processes are stimulated or triggered by internal needs that are aroused. Just what the needs are is still a subject of much discussion and study.

- Motivation is action directed toward specific goals intended to satisfy needs. These goals are not necessarily the most desirable or appropriate goals from the manager's viewpoint, but they are voluntarily chosen by a person because they will satisfy a need.

- Motivation is not the same as performance; it is a description of behaviors, such as working quickly to stock shelves or making a certain number of sales calls. The fact that you are motivated, of course, does not mean that you are stocking the shelves correctly or closing sales.

Your challenge is to motivate your employees to do their best work. By understanding some of the basic theories of motivation, you will be better prepared to find the "carrot and stick" combination that works with your employees. Again, you need to find ways to align your employee's self-interests with the interests of the company. This challenge is depicted in Figure 6-1.

There is no management approach applicable to all situations; likewise, theories of motivation each have distinct differences. In this section, we will examine three of the major theories about work motivation that are the roots of many contemporary management techniques: the needs theory, the motivation-hygiene theory, and the expectancy theory. We will then look at how these theories can be applied to influence employee motivation. Don't be overwhelmed by these theories; they are simply

FIGURE 6-1   Managers Must Align Employees' Personal
Goals and Needs with Those of the Company.

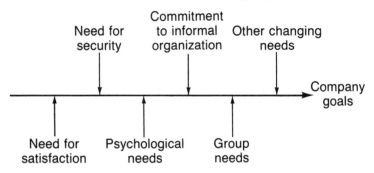

different ways of thinking about why employees do
what they do, and any additional thinking we can
do about this topic is useful!

Needs Theories

Abraham Maslow, one of the pioneer behavioral
scientists, introduced his hierarchy-of-needs theory
in 1943. According to Maslow's theory, people are
motivated by needs they want to satisfy. He grouped
needs into five distinct types: physiological, safety,
social, esteem (recognition and status), and self-
fulfillment (realization of one's unique and complete
potential) needs. These needs are hierarchical, or arranged in the sequence in which they must be basically satisfied.

Maslow's theory of human motivation is based on
the following assumptions:

- Needs that are not satisfied motivate or influence
  behavior.

- As long as needs are unsatisfied, they monopolize a person's consciousness and have almost exclusive power to motivate behavior.
- As soon as needs are satisfied, they lose the power to motivate.
- Needs are satisfied according to a hierarchy of importance. The lowest level of unmet needs must be basically, but not competely, satisfied before the next level of needs becomes important enough to have the power to motivate.

Social scientist David McClelland suggests that secondary needs determine behavior and augment Maslow's universal needs. McClelland's needs theory is concerned with how individual needs and environmental factors combine to form three basic motives:

- the need for achievement
- the need for power
- the need for affiliation

According to McClelland's theory, each of these three motives evokes a different sense of satisfaction. Everyone has each motive in varying degrees, but one motive is dominant in most situations and characterize most of a person's behavior.

McClelland says that because these motives explain most behavior, employees can be categorized and motivated accordingly. The probability that a person will perform a job effectively depends upon a combination of

- the strength of the motive or need relative to other needs,

- the possibility of success in performing the task,
- and the strength value of the incentive or reward for performance.

Managers find it useful in recruitment and selection of personnel to understand that certain jobs are best performed by persons predisposed to a particular motivation. For example, to the extent that a job requires calculated risk-taking and rigorous goal-setting behavior, an achievement-motivated person will do better than a power-oriented or affiliation-oriented person. Likewise, if the successful performance of a job requires cooperation, an affiliation-motivated person will do the best job. If the job requires influencing others, and all other factors are equal, a person oriented toward power will be most successful.

Motivation-Hygiene Theory

Another motivation theory that many managers have found useful is Fredrick Herzberg's motivation-hygiene theory. Herzberg found that the aspects of people's jobs that made them feel good or satisfied were factors intrinsic to the job itself. These factors included achievement, recognition, work itself, responsibility, advancement, and personal growth. Herzberg called these sources of satisfaction motivators, because they apparently were necessary for substantial improvements in work performance.

Herzberg also found that when people described why and when they were dissatisfied with their jobs, many talked about conditions surrounding their jobs rather than the job itself. Some of the factors mentioned were company policy and administration, their relationship with their supervisor, work conditions, salary, relationships with peers, relationships with subordinates, personal problems, status, and security. Herzberg called these sources of dissatisfaction hygiene or maintenance factors because they form the work environment, rather than the work itself.

According to Herzberg, satisfaction and dissatisfaction are not opposite ends of the same continuum; rather, they are entirely separate dimensions that must be dealt with in different ways. Satisfaction is affected by motivators (those factors relating to the job content), and dissatisfaction is affected by hygiene or maintenance factors (those factors relating to the job environment). Note that removing negative hygiene factors does not automatically heighten motivation. It does clear the way for one or more motivators to have a positive effect.

Herzberg is generally credited with the concept of job enrichment as a motivator. This concept has been successfully modified and applied by many organizations to be an effective tool to raise performance through increased motivation.

Expectancy Theory

The needs theories do not adequately account for differences in individual employees or explain why people behave in certain ways. The valence-instrumentality-expectancy theory is based on what the employee believes about his behavior and what he perceives as important or of value. The key concepts of the expectancy theory are that motivation depends on

1. the belief that a person's effort will result in performance—referred to as expectancy,

2. the belief that a person's performance will be rewarded—referred to as instrumentality,

3. the perceived value a person places on a specific outcome—referred to as valence.

According to the expectancy theory, all these factors—expectancy, instrumentality, and valence of rewards—must be present so that a high level of motivation can occur.

The manager's goal should be to provide outcomes that subordinates value highly and to ensure that they perceive a high probability of those outcomes occurring if they behave as desired.

A Final Theory: The Contingency Approach

The optimistic aspect of contemporary management is that there are no built-in reasons why work cannot be pleasant and satisfying or why employees' constructive work behavior cannot be encouraged. However, the unpredictability of employee responses to the work environment suggests that a combination of motivational theories may be most effective in a specific situation or at a particular work site. A healthy measure of common sense and prac-

Figure 6-2
Expectancy: the "thinking" side of motivation.

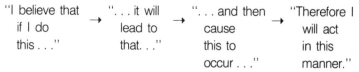

| "I believe that if I do this . . ." | → | ". . . it will lead to that. . ." | → | ". . . and then cause this to occur . . ." | → | "Therefore I will act in this manner." |

The expectancy theory suggests that wants and needs are not enough to motivate behavior. Rather, motivation stems from the belief that a combination of interconnected events will achieve a desired result.

tical experience drawn from that which has yielded positive results in the past should also be added. This results-oriented approach is commonly referred to as the *contingency approach.*

The contingency approach acknowledges that there is no single best management philosophy that is equally accurate or effective in all circumstances. No plans, organizational structures, influencing techniques or controls will fit all situations. Instead, managers must find unique ways to be effective in each situation.

The contingency approach urges avoidance of any unthinking, wholesale application of a single philosophy. Instead, the manager should engage in healthy experimentation within the guidelines of the main theories, and embrace the pragmatic solutions that work better than any others. Motivating employees means identifying those needs that will cause employees to act, and then clearly communicating the probability that those needs will be satisfied when employees contribute their efforts toward accomplishing organizational tasks.

GETTING RESULTS THROUGH LEADERSHIP

An understanding of motivation theory does not automatically translate into motivated employees. After the needs of the employees have been identified, or the motivators have been selected, someone has to speak up and communicate the organizational objectives. You, as a company leader, are that person; you have to make something happen by exercising influencing skills in your position as a leader.

Leadership causes others to do what the leader wants them to do. It is a combination of personal characteristics that earn for a person the privilege of influencing a group more than anyone else. A good leader is one who motivates others to put forth their best efforts.

Leaders can come by their leadership skills intuitively, but leadership can also be learned. Lee Iacocca, the leader of the Chrysler recovery in the early 1980s, certainly has the ability to inspire others and draw from them extraordinary performance. But, like other strong leaders, Iacocca's skills go beyond charisma. He has learned what motivates individual workers and uses this knowledge to direct their activities.

Power of the Leader

Every group has a leader, and that person's leadership begins with power. A leader's source of power logically reinforces his or her position of greatest influence; after all, it is the leaders of groups who usually control the distribution of resources, rewards, and punishments. Leaders also control the duties and assignments made to specific people, and they often select basic group goals. Given this authority, it is not surprising that other group members orient themselves toward and readily accept influence from leaders.

A leader's power comes from one or both of two sources: traditional power sources that depend on the person's position within the organization and personal power sources that are based on personal characteristics recognized by group members.

Traditional or positional power attributed to a leader is signaled by a specific position or title. This source of power stays with the position; whoever carries that title has the power that goes with it. It is typically oriented downward on the organizational chart, can be delegated and works best with tasks that do not require specific individuals to complete them.

Personal power is much more likely to be associated with a natural or intuitive leader who may lack an official position, but nevertheless earns an informal position of influence. Personal power travels with a person because it is based on personal characteristics. If a person with personal power moves to a new position or joins a new committee, he manages to influence the group involved almost immediately because of the power he brings with them. Personal power is oriented upward on the organizational chart and works equally well with tasks and people. Personal power is generally regarded as stronger than positional power, and when the two clash, personal power usually wins.

Power is limited by the type or types of power that the leader has. We first discussed power in

Chapter 5 (see Figure 5-2) in the context of the informal organization. Here's how you can influence the informal organization to your advantage.

A leader can have more than one of the following five bases of power, but they must be acquired in the order presented to avoid the abuse of power or a lack of credibility.

- *Expert power.* Managers have expert power to the extent that subordinates or others attribute knowledge and expertise to them. If you are regarded as a subject-matter expert only, you are limited to leadership in only well-defined areas, such as engineering or the personnel department, but not both.
- *Positional power.* Group members believe that a leader with a defined position above them in the organization ought to have power over them. A top manager newly transferred, for example, will expect to have the power incumbent with the position.
- *Referent power.* When a leader has referent power, group members identify with or want to be like him or her and therefore do what the manager wants out of a sense of respect, liking, and wanting to be liked. These leaders are often described as charismatic.
- *Reward power.* A leader has reward power over group members if he or she has the ability to deliver positive consequences (such as letting people leave work early) or remove negative consequences (such as improve working conditions) in response to their behavior.
- *Coercive power.* A leader has coercive power over other group members if he can mete out

negative consequences (such as reprimands, demotions, or extra work assignments) or remove positive consequences (such as blocking promotions) in response to the behavior of group members.

Leadership is not management. A good manager is a good leader, but a good leader is not necessarily a successful manager. Managers are generally associated with administrative, technical, and verbal skills, whereas leaders have strong interpersonal, coaching, counseling, and advocacy skills. Leaders also are acknowledged change agents within an organization because they have sufficient personal power to introduce new ideas and persuade others to try them. The effective leader understands his base and source of power and uses a leadership style appropriate to the situation, to those he seeks to lead, and his relative position within the group.

Leadership Styles

Because leaders are highly visible within every organization, they have received more than their fair share of scrutiny. Researchers and management theorists generally agree that there are four basic leadership styles:

1. Autocratic leaders tell subordinates what to do and expect to be obeyed without question. The autocratic leader assumes he will have to coerce, control, or threaten employees in order to motivate them. Their strength is their decisiveness; their weakness is the failure to maximize the strengths of subordinates.

2. Participative leaders involve subordinates in decisions but retain final authority. They share a strong mutual respect with their subordinates for each other's technical expertise and input. Participative leaders assume that employees desire greater responsibility in the organization. This style enhances job satisfaction, but slows the decision-making process.

3. Democratic leaders try to do what the majority of subordinates desire. They value consensus above efficiency, and rely on rationality and thorough explanations to influence the group.

4. Laissez-faire leaders are uninvolved with the work of the group. This appears to work only with groups that are highly expert and well-motivated so that the need for leadership is minimized, such as with groups of scientists.

Because of the manager's position in the organization, the manager's leadership style can do much to establish the attitudes and work habits of the work group he or she supervises. There are exceptions, of course, but the employees usually reflect the manager's style. The manager's assumptions about his employees and his relationship with them has a profound effect on the management policies, communication patterns, and quality of work environment in the organization.

Assumptions about how others will behave actually affects how they behave. This is called the con-

Figure 6-3
Alternate Leadership Styles: Advantages and Disadvantages.

	Advantages	*Disadvantages*
Autocratic	• Improves productivity • Helpful in high-pressure situations • Speeds decision-making process	• Does not make the most of employees' ideas or skills • Reduces employee job satisfaction
Participative	• Raises employee job satisfaction • Fosters strong commitment to organization • Preferred by most employees	• Slows decision-making process • Raises doubts about the leader's competence and/or strength
Democratic	• Value placed on reaching consensus ensures complete discussion of decisions • The best idea usually wins	• Least efficient • Begs the question, "Whose decision is this?" • Group process can be manipulative
Laissez-faire	• Expects and recognizes competence and motivation of employees • Nurtures individual contributions and creativity	• Unsettling for people who want or need structure • Possible deficiencies in communication within and between work groups

cept of self-fulfilling prophecy and is summarized in four principles:

1. Managers (and everyone else, too!) hold certain assumptions and expectations of people or events.

2. These assumptions and expectations are communicated to others via various cues.

3. People tend to respond to these cues by adjusting their behavior to match them.

4. The result is that the original expectation becomes true, thus reinforcing the original expectation and creating a cycle of self-fulfilling prophecies.

The following theories provide a framework for discussing leadership style and its impact on the productivity of the organization.

Theory X and Theory Y

Two opposing philosophies of human nature at work have been differentiated by management theorist Douglas McGregor. Traditional management assumptions about workers have been grouped together loosely and comprise Theory X.

The Theory X philosophy of management assumes that workers are by nature selfish, lazy, lacking in ambition, reluctant to assume responsibility and indifferent to organizational needs. In other words, the Theory X approach presumes that most or all workers are by nature unmotivated to work.

If a manager subscribes to this pessimistic philosophy, his management techniques are likely to reflect his distrust of worker's motives and his generally low expectations for worker performance.

Figure 6-4
Theory X and Theory Y Offer Alternate Assumptions
About Employees.

Theory X	*Theory Y*
• Most people dislike work, work only because they believe they have to, and avoid it if possible. • Most people lack responsibility. • Most people lack ambition. • Most people seek security above all. • Most people must be coerced, controlled, and threatened with punishment in order to work. • With these assumptions, Theory X managers seek results by coercing and controlling employees.	• Most people want to do good work and be recognized for it. • Work is as natural as play or rest. • Most people want to be well managed. • Most people exercise self-direction and self-control in the service of objectives to which they are committed. • Most people have potential. They seek and accept responsibility under the proper conditions. They have imagination, ingenuity, and creativity that can be applied to work. • With these assumptions, Theory Y managers seek results by creating work environments that develop the potential of employees.

This suggests that the Theory X manager must coerce, control, or threaten employees in order to motivate them. This philosophy has prevailed for centuries and is still very common today.

The more optimistic philosophy of human nature at work is called Theory Y. This is often referred to as the human relations approach to management. Supporters of Theory Y assume that workers are not passive participants in the organization's development, and, because of their basic nature, workers desire increasing amounts of responsibility and skill development in accordance with the organization's needs.

The Theory Y philosophy makes some assumptions about management, too. The human relations approach depends on supportive management practices that enable workers to develop their own potential. It also depends on the workers to bring a team-oriented attitude to their jobs.

Theory X and Theory Y are neither good nor bad; they are simply effective or ineffective in specific situations. The following theories offer similarly useful frameworks that help the manager think about leadership.

The Managerial Grid® by Robert Blake and Jane Mouton

The Managerial Grid has gained wide acceptance as a useful diagnostic tool for ailing management systems that need to see themselves from an entirely new perspective. The Managerial Grid is a two-dimensional matrix that relates a manager's concern for people (vertical axis) with his or her concern for production or task completion (horizontal axis). The grid is 9 × 9; the higher the number, the higher the level of concern. Through a series of questions, the management style can be plotted and visually portrayed.

The Managerial Grid depicts five major leadership styles:

FIGURE 6-5 The Manager Must Balance Concern for People with Concern for Production

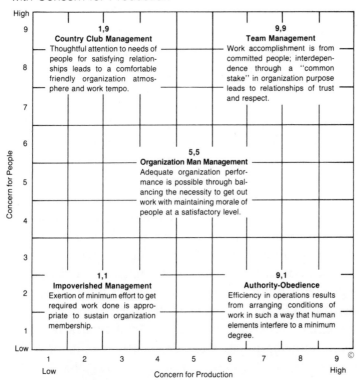

SOURCE The Managerial Grid® figure from *The Managerial Grid III: The Key to Leadership Excellence,* by Robert R. Blake and Jane Srygley Mouton. Houston: Gulf Publishing Company, Copyright © 1985, page 12. Reproduced by permission.

- *1,1 Impoverished management.* The manager has little concern for either people or production.
- *9,1 Authority-obedience management.* The manager stresses efficient operation through controls and tries to minimize situations in which people can interfere. This manager wants production at any cost.
- *1,9 Country club management.* The manager is thoughtful, comfortable, and friendly, and very likely to try for consensus. Little concern for output.
- *5,5 Organization man management.* The manager attempts to balance and trade off concern for tasks in exchange for a satisfactory level of morale. This manager is a compromiser.
- *9,9 Team management.* The manager seeks high output through committed people; he has high expectations in terms of mutual trust, respect, and interdependence.

Since Blake and Mouton introduced the Managerial Grid in the early 1960s, they have suggested that the 9,9 team management position is the most effective. The reasons are self-evident: A high concern for output or people which does not compromise the other axis yields highly satisfied employees who are highly productive. They present the grid as a way of visualizing the current and desired position of the leadership team. At the very least, it can raise the expectations the manager sets for himself, thereby laying the groundwork for a new "self-fulfilling prophecy."

Leadership Continuum

The leadership continuum is the graphic represen-
tation of the exchanges that occur between a
manager's use of authority and the freedom that
subordinates experience as leadership styles shift
from boss-centered to employee-centered. The
model was developed by Robert Tannenbaum and
Warren H. Schmidt and depicts a series of factors
that they think influence a manager's selection of
the most appropriate leadership style.

Here is how the leadership continuum model
works: As the manager gives up his authority, the
subordinate accepts additional freedom. For example, a manager may use a more participative leadership style when subordinates

- seek independence,
- understand and are committed to the goals of
  the organization,
- are well-educated and experienced in performing the jobs,
- seek responsibility for decision making,
- expect a participative style of leadership.

When these conditions do not exist, the manager
may need to adopt a more autocratic leadership
style. The most effective managers are neither task-
centered nor people-centered, but flexible enough
to respond to different situations with a variable
style that is predisposed to share as much authority
with the employee as the employee is prepared to
accept.

Which Leadership Style Is Best?

Given that many approaches to leadership are learned in the process of becoming an effective manager, the desire for a single best leadership style is understandable. However, as we have already seen in other areas of management, there is no single best answer.

Most theorists agree that a model must accommodate the differences among situations and the differences among leaders in order to be useful. Factors affecting the choice of leadership style include the manager's philosophy of human nature, experiences, training, and professional and technical competence. Similarly, the workers' belief system, attitudes toward work and authority, maturity level, experience, and skill level affect the leadership style that is most effective.

Even more factors are related to the situation that affects the leadership style, including

1. Number of people in the work group

2. Types of tasks

3. Situational stress

4. Objectives of the unit

5. Presence or absence of a union

6. Leadership style of the manager's boss

7. Overall relationship of the manager with the subordinates.

THE PAYOFF: INCREASED PRODUCTIVITY

It is hard work to motivate and lead employees. Not only does it require considerable skill development on the part of the manager, but it may also be personally exhausting. Remember that the manager is working in a fluid social environment inside the organization, an environment that can never be fully controlled. By the nature of his job, he has to be prepared to respond to many eventualities, shifting his leadership style in the process.

Is it worth it? On a personal level, most managers probably feel that it is. Their needs for recognition and self-fulfillment are partially met by being effective in their job, and they have the satisfaction of seeing their plans and visions for the organization amplified through the efforts of others.

Improved productivity for the organization is the greatest benefit. A skilled manager with the ability to motivate and lead others can dramatically improve the output of an organization without increasing costs simply by maximizing the human resources.

Volvo has put new motivation and leadership ideas to work on a large scale at their automobile plant in Kalmar, Sweden. A new managing director interpreted the 41 percent annual turnover rate (in spite of high salaries) to mean that the workers did not like their jobs. Indeed, on closer inspection, he learned that highly educated employees were being asked to perform increasingly monotonous, tedious jobs. They didn't feel good about themselves, and they were frustrated with the company. The manager suspected that many quality problems stemmed from the employees' poor performance caused by negative feelings.

By adopting a highly participative leadership style, the manager involved key employee leaders in the plant's productivity and quality problems. Doubtful at first that their suggestions would be taken seriously, the employees soon became committed to redesigning the assembly line as a solution to both problems. The result was a new plant with a lot of new ideas and fresh enthusiasm. The old assembly line with one person doing one task all day was replaced by 25 work teams consisting of 15 to 25 workers. Each team was responsible for one aspect of production, such as the electrical system. As long as the team met the production quota, they could organize themselves in any way they liked. Job rotation became commonplace.

Combined with other employee-centered design features like windows, music, and quieter work environments, turnover plummeted, training costs dropped, productivity began to rise, and quality ceased to be a problem. Why? Because the employees were treated with respect and given an opportunity to participate in decisions that affected their workplace. Although the plant was not a democracy, it was a far cry from the product-centered management style of the manager's predecessor. The production requirements stayed the same, but now the workers could decide how the job was to get done.

Volvo and many other firms are seeking new ways to lead, motivate, and manage employees in order to achieve higher productivity.

SUMMARY

Motivation and leadership, coupled with effective communication techniques, are the most powerful tools available for the manager available for the manager seeking to influence the actions and performance of subordinates. The quality of a manager's influence is reflected in the productivity of the organization.

Understanding motivation means understanding the needs of the employees. Their reasons are not always clear, even to themselves, but the manager must nevertheless seek ways to give employees meaningful reasons to perform their jobs effectively and efficiently. Maslow's hierarchy of needs, McClelland's socially acquired needs, Herzberg's hygiene-motivator theory, and the valence-instrumentality-expectancy theory all suggest different ways of looking at the same fundamental challenge.

The manager's challenge remains to work through others by influencing their actions and behaviors. Planning and organizing functions are not enough to achieve the organization's objectives. By themselves, they are little more than good intentions and theoretical exercises. Only by motivating and leading subordinates to high performance actions can a manager succeed.

7

Controlling Skills

Controlling is the fourth management function after planning, organizing, and influencing. Broadly speaking, controlling is the process of comparing actual performance with planned performance, and then correcting or reinforcing the actual performance. There are three basic steps to this process:

1. the establishment of standards

2. the evaluation of performance

3. the correction or reinforcement of performance that is below or above the standards

The control process is interrelated with the planning function in two important ways. Controlling activities begin at the planning stage when specific performance standards are written into objectives. Objectives that specify results in units of measure, such as quantity, time, distance, or a budget, are essentially expressing performance standards. For example, when a manager of a lawn care company sets as an objective the servicing of five lawns per person per day, he is actually establishing a standard of performance for his crew members.

The second significant interaction between planning and control occurs when the actual performance is compared with the planned performance. If the actual performance is acceptable, there is no need to change the plan. But if the actual performance is significantly higher or lower than the established performance standard, the plan must be updated to reflect the more realistic standards. In the example just mentioned, the manager of the lawn care crew must revise his schedule of commitments and his cash flow projections if he observes a lower-than-expected servicing rate per day. If the plan is not kept current as the management cycle repeats itself, the planning function loses its credibility and usefulness.

The control function should be regarded as a feedback and forecasting tool. Effective control mechanisms alert the manager to problems before they occur or before they become too serious to correct. By comparing actual performance with planned performance, problems with scheduling, delivery of raw materials, quality, budgeting, production volumes, and the like are readily apparent. If the manager can see a problem developing within 30 or 60 days or more in the future, he or she may still have enough time to take corrective action. Likewise, if a new idea or star employee is performing better than expected, the appropriate reinforcement can be provided while there is still enough time to maximize this type of opportunity. In short, controls help managers to avoid expensive surprises.

STEP ONE: ESTABLISHING STANDARDS

The concept of control is rooted in the standards decided on during the planning phase. Standards provide a reference point against which performance can be measured. Without clearly understanding what is expected before the work is started, neither the manager nor the subordinate will know what is considered to be acceptable performance. In other words, without standards, how can an employee's performance be evaluated? With what would it be compared? The setting of meaningful standards as control points when plans are made is an important link between these two management functions.

Quantifiable standards are the most useful. Standards expressed in terms of costs, revenues, products produced, time to complete, net profit, unit sales, dividends, and the like are easily monitored by the manager and the subordinate. Target numbers and time frames can be attached to each of these numbers. Interim standards can usually be devised, too, such as, "Finish the initial design phase of the new building by the first of next month," or "Complete the inventory and restocking phase by Friday." Again, if the standards highlight key control points in the work flow, the manager will be able to identify major problems before they occur.

FIGURE 7-1 Steps Leading to Control

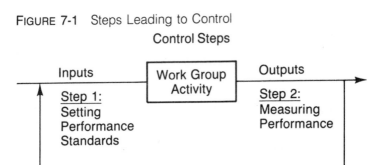

Some situations defy quantifiable standards, however. As work becomes less technical, it becomes increasingly difficult to find objective criteria to represent the work in a meaningful way. What standards could be used to measure the improvement of employee morale? How would a top-level manager's performance be evaluated? Standards that are indirectly related to the objective usually can be found, but these are imprecise measurements of performance. Employee morale, for example, may be judged to be improved because of a reduced rate of absenteeism, and a senior manager may be praised because the company's profitability is up by several percentage points. But these standards are only attempts to measure the unmeasurable by inference. Against what standards would a person measure an employee's motivation? On what basis would a public relations effort be judged a success?

Standards are most meaningful when they are set with input from those whose performance is being measured. The employees doing the work are likely to have sound suggestions for the best control points. They also will be more confident that the evaluation process if fair if they take part in its construction.

STEP TWO: EVALUATING PERFORMANCE

The manager evaluates the performance of his subordinates by comparing actual performance to the standards established during the planning stage and determining if deviations from the standards merit corrective or reinforcing action. Fair evaluation depends on the accurate measurement of actual performance at the same control points specified by the standards. In other words, actual performance should be expressed in the same terms and units as the standards.

Many measurements and comparisons will be straightforward, but frequently they will vary from the standard by a slight amount. Most of the time, this small variance has no effect on the end result and should be overlooked. The amount of the acceptable variation is called the *tolerance*. For example, the manager of an overnight photoprocessing service may expect 100 percent of all orders in by 5:00 P.M. to be ready for customer pickup by 10:00 A.M. the following morning; if the manager is satisfied when 95 percent of the orders are ready, he allows a five percent tolerance. The supervisor on a packaging line may set 50 units per minute as the standard, but will allow a variance or tolerance between 47 and 53 units.

By accepting work within predetermined tolerances, the manager acknowledges that circumstances beyond the employees' control can skew short-term performance. Experienced managers know that, practically speaking, no one can be perfect or uniformly consistent all the time. Instead of wasting time analyzing minor deviations of no consequence, they apply the *exception principle,* which focuses their attention on those situations with particularly good or particularly bad performance.

When performance is less mechanical and less specific, it is more difficult to measure. This is particularly true with milestones or benchmarks for work-in-progress, which can be subjective and indistinct. A research technician or advertising designer, for example, may find it impossible to judge how far from the correct answer or correct design he is. He may know how many experiments he's tried and how many hours he has put into the project, but he cannot say whether he is one-third or three-quarters of the way toward the solution. This difficulty occurs often enough in most organizations to be a problem, thus reinforcing the trend toward selecting more quantitative standards in the planning stage whenever possible.

STEP THREE: TAKING CORRECTIVE OR REINFORCING ACTION

After actual performance is compared with the standards set up in the original plan, the manager must decide whether a performance gap exists. If the actual results meet or exceed the planned results, the decision is easy: compliment the employee on a job well done and give him or her some well-deserved recognition. If the superlative performance continues, as it might with the proper reinforcement, the manager should analyze the reasons behind the success. Perhaps the employee has developed a new technique that can be taught to others doing the same job; or, perhaps the difference is because of improved tools or new component parts or simply a better attitude toward the work. The only risk in this situation is spoiling the good performance with indifference or with unwarranted meddling. By not acknowledging the good performance or by "fixing something that isn't broken," the employee may believe that extra effort doesn't matter and return to mediocre performance.

On the other hand, if a performance gap exists, the manager is obliged to take corrective action. This requires some problem solving on the manager's part. Failure to achieve desired results cannot be automatically assumed to be the fault of the employee. Was the plan sound, or was it asking for too much in too short a time? Were the standards realistic, or were they "best guesses" based on unrelated experiences or insufficient information? Did the person assigned to this task have all the time and resources originally allocated to him or her, or did someone else's assignment conflict with his and cause a scheduling problem? Was he given the leadership and motivation he needed? Did he understand the importance of the project? Did he have an opportunity to communicate with the rest of the team assigned to this project?

Obviously, the manager's problem-solving efforts are going to be more successful if the worker is involved in the analysis. The experienced manager will be positive and constructive in this discussion. It is possible that something happened that made the successful completion of the plan more difficult. A worker's failure to communicate problems that made the plan unworkable is a very different problem than failure to perform. The prudent manager will keep in mind that the long-term objective is not to assign blame, but to accomplish the original objectives. This employee is probably going to be the one finishing the assignment after the plan is modified. If he is treated fairly by the manager, his attitude and performance will be much better.

After the cause of the performance gap is identified, corrective actions can be taken. Ideally, the manager can control the cause of the problem and bring the performance back into line to match the original plan. A corrective technique to start with is simple feedback to the employee. Describing, but not evaluating, the performance gap to the employee responsible often makes enough of an impression to correct the problem. This nonjudgmental feedback is a form of performance counseling.

There are other corrective actions to try. Additional or remedial training can correct skill deficiencies; tools and equipment can be repaired or upgraded; motivational techniques can be tried; and new people with more experience can be assigned to do the work.

Remedies like this do not always work, however, because many circumstances are beyond the manager's control. Late deliveries of materials by outside vendors, strikes, poor marketing results, a downturn in the economy, and pressure from a new competitor are examples of circumstances beyond the control of the manager, which can have a negative effect on employee performance. In these situations, the manager must change the plan to reflect the new reality.

When the control system of an organization is effective, it helps management focus on deviations from the standards prescribed in the plan. It is at once a feedback mechanism for signaling above- or below-average performance, a diagnostic process for solving the problem, and a feedback system that updates the plan so that it can continue to forecast the organization's future.

OTHER CHARACTERISTICS OF AN EFFECTIVE CONTROL SYSTEM

A control system cannot be constructed overnight. It is unique to every organization, and it is only as strong and effective as the participant's desire to improve.

The two most important characteristics, objectivity and tolerance, were discussed previously. Other important characteristics that make a control system effective are listed below.

Information availability and pertinence. The control system provides only the information necessary to make decisions. Control systems can be paralyzed by too much information on the wrong type of information. The manager and employees must decide early in the planning process what information should be collected. Collecting information that will not be used in a meaningful way is wasted effort and an administrative nightmare.

Timeliness. Prompt reporting of performance gives the organization the best opportunities to respond and update the planning process. In addition, the participants feel more confident and involved in the process if they receive timely feedback.

Flexibility. As the plan is updated, the control system must also be updated. If the controlling mechanisms are allowed to become outdated, they will not be able to provide results when they are really needed.

Economy. Administering a control system costs time and money, and it must be worth the effort. It is inherently difficult to measure the precise dollar and cent value of most control measures after they have been implemented. For this reason, it is important to measure the key factors before and after a new control measure is implemented. Most successful systems grow naturally, one component at a time. Those features that prove to be worthwhile are continued, and those that turn out to be too time-consuming, too confusing, too expensive, or too trivial are discarded.

CONTROL TECHNIQUES

There are many types of control techniques. The challenge for the manager is to find the type best suited to his or her situation and then adapt it to meet a specific set of needs. Most control techniques can be described simply as tools or mechanisms for communicating specific information to the people who need it at the time they need it. A few examples are listed below:

> *Budgets.* Budgets are familiar to everyone who has to administer household finances. A business uses a budget in the same way, as a guide to avoid spending more than it ought to. Like a good plan, a good budget is specific, itemizing the limits within which certain purchases must be made. Typically, a budget has two columns: one column presents the amount budgeted for an expense item, such as long distance telephone calls or legal fees; the column next to it is the amount actually spent. This format makes it possible to quickly check the soundness of the budgeting process, which in turn strengthens or weakens management's confidence in the financial plan.

> *Expense records.* Expense records are a reporting tool, not a planning tool. The important aspect of expense records is the documentation. They work as a control mechanism because the documentation makes it possible to keep track of and justify certain types of expenditures that otherwise would be outside the normal purchase ordering system. Expense records are commonly kept for business travel and entertainment costs.

> *Gantt chart.* The Gantt chart is a graphic depiction of work progress as it relates to a time frame. Ideally, separate tasks can be identified

and plotted side-by-side on the chart to show how they relate to each other. Some tasks can be performed simultaneously; others cannot be started until others are completed. In the Gantt chart, the beginning time and ending time for each task is estimated. With a quick glance, a person can gauge whether the work is on schedule or not. The Gantt chart is popular as a project planning tool.

Many other control techniques communicate specific information, including financial ratios, quality control reports, behavior analyses, break-even point analyses, what-if financial projections, milestone schedules, critical path charts, program evaluation and review technique (PERT) charts, strategic control points, and many others. Many of these are self-explanatory; it is important to remember that the manager's duty is to assign control techniques that are suitable to the organization's plans.

OVERCOMING NEGATIVE REACTIONS TO CONTROLS

As important as controls are to the company, it cannot be assumed that the employees share this view. Quite the contrary, many employees have a knee-jerk negative response to the introduction of control mechanisms. It is natural to resist efforts to control a person's freedom, even if it can be argued that the controls directly benefit the organization that is a person's livelihood. Prolonged or rising resistance to controls, however, suggests that the controls should be reappraised for suitability. Answering the following five questions will help you reappraise the controls.

1. *Are the controls understandable?* If standards or procedures are not clear, frustration can occur. Employees know that if they do not understand what is expected of them, their performance probably will not be satisfactory. The manager needs to go further than vague encouragement about "improving customer satisfaction" and communicate to the employees the specific measurements that he will be watching.

2. *Are the controls realistic?* Establishing unworkable objectives or unattainable goals is short-sighted. The function of a set of controls is to change performance so that results will be those that were planned. If employees sense that controls are completely unrealistic, they will not try to attain them, thus undermining the credibility of the control system altogether.

3. *Are the controls timely?* The significance of a poor decision made by an assembly technician is lost if he does not get prompt feedback. Routine actions are quickly forgotten, particularly if there is no apparent reason to remember them. If the control system is to be effective, it has to communicate deviations from the expected performance as quickly as practical.

4. *Are the controls understood to be justifiable?* Controls that are imposed without explanation are likely to be viewed as repressive. Because the employees are expected to be full participants in the control system, they are entitled to understand how a particular two-person "buddy system" in a laboratory, for example, directly affects the quality of product, the profitability of the firm, and the long-term job stability of everyone else.

5. *Are the controls accurate?* Even under the best circumstances, it is natural for employees to view the causes of their performance deficiencies differently from that of management. "That's not the way it happened" is a common response. If an employee is confronted with performance data that he suspects to be inaccurate, he will begin to distrust the control process. If an employee consistently finds errors in the data used to make decisions, it is appropriate to suspect the accuracy of all evaluations.

SUMMARY

Planning and control are not free-standing activities, independent of each other and the other functions of management. Nor are they performed as an afterthought following disappointing performance. They are closely interrelated, forming a continuous loop of performance guidance and performance feedback. The performance guidance is in the form of plans and performance standards; the feedback is in the form of evaluation and corrective action.

To manage means to achieve the organization's objectives through the efforts of others. Managers at all levels of the organization are essentially problem solvers and decision makers. With the right control mechanisms in place, they can focus on the exceptionally high or low performance situations. Under some circumstances, the performance gap can be remedied with additional training or performance counseling; when this is not possible, the company's plans must be updated to reflect the now-known reality.

8

Communicating About Performance

The managerial skills we've discussed so far—planning, organizing, influencing, and controlling—help you improve the organization's productivity and profitability. These four managerial skills can get most people doing mostly acceptable work. But by themselves, they are not enough. These skills will only yield modest success until you use your one-to-one interpersonal communication skills to talk with your people about their performance.

You communicate about performance throughout the processes of planning, organizing, influencing, and controlling. Your communication skills lubricate and link all these processes, making your push toward improved performance either more or less effective.

In your position, you hold a lot of power to affect the performance of your workers. What you say and don't say about their current performance, both good and bad, determines what their future performance will be. You should regard every discussion you have about performance as an opportunity to develop your workers.

Communicating about good performance is difficult, perhaps because we believe that we should speak up only when someone does something wrong, fearful that anything we say will jeopardize the status quo. We are much more used to "catching someone doing something bad" than "catching them doing something good."

Communicating about poor performance is also difficult. It means you are going to have to give someone bad news ("I'm sorry, this is not working out."), make the person feel uncomfortable ("You lied to me, and I want an explanation."), or even tell him or her to grow up ("Your irresponsible behavior is causing a problem. This has to stop now.").

No matter how difficult it is, communicating about performance is one of your most important jobs because employees want and need to know how they are doing, clearly and fairly, so they can continue to learn and grow.

YOUR RESPONSIBILITIES

As the leader of your work group, your responsibility is to direct your employees and maximize their work efforts. This means that you will have to do your best to develop your employees' potential and evaluate their progress. These activties take the form of:

- Informal feedback about performance (often called coaching or counseling conversations),
- Formal feedback about performance (often called performance reviews),
- Evaluations and recommendations about the readiness of an employee for advancement, a raise, a transfer, new assignments, and so on, which help the company best use the skills and abilities of this person.

You now have a large responsibility for the success of your employees. Their jobs and careers depend on how well you rate their performance. This is a wonderful opportunity for you to help them develop by giving them feedback about their performance. Your opinion means a lot to them; make the most of the opportunities you have to guide them. The managers rated highest by employees are those who help them become the best they can be.

The bottom line, then, is that you are in the best position to evaluate, and therefore improve, your employees' performance because you can provide lots of informal and formal feedback. The best way to do this is within the context of a performance management system, either the company's or one of your own design.

By following a performance management system, you can do the following:

Stay in touch.   Much of your feedback about performance will be informal communication, both verbal and written. A performance management system provides you with some of the language and tools that will make this communication easier and clearer. For example, you can request an employee to join you for "an informal performance discussion about the Allied project" without sending confusing signals. An informal discussion is usually an off-the-record update of work-in-progress, but it is more serious than a casual conversation at the water cooler.

Stay organized. Are you meeting with your people frequently enough? You should have at least one formal performance review every year, preferably two. If you are supervising six to eight people, you may be conducting a formal review with someone every three to five weeks.

Document progress. It's difficult to track improvement and development if you don't write it down. Select or devise an evaluation form that meets your need to document performance objectives and progress toward those objectives. Then, when you meet with an employee, you will be able to discuss specific performance problems or improvements. It is likely that you will use these records to make your case for giving this person a raise, an award, or a promotion.

Document problems. If performance improvement is not forthcoming, you will need a "paper trail" that documents your efforts to give the employee ample opportunity to correct the problem. Disciplinary action, termination, not giving a raise, not promoting—all these decisions will have to be defended, and it will be much easier to explain your reasoning if you are well documented.

Develop the employee. This is the greatest benefit of a performance management system because it helps you and your employee plan his or her development. Right there, in black and white, is the plan that both of you understand and believe in. It highlights strengths and weaknesses, priorities for performance improvement, career objectives—whatever is meaningful to both of you. It serves as a trusty compass when either of you are tempted to become distracted or pursue a conflicting objective.

SUGGESTIONS FOR GIVING FEEDBACK

Because it is unreasonable to expect an employee to improve his performance when he thinks it is acceptable, you have to let him know otherwise. Providing feedback about performance lets a person know how well he is doing his job.

To provide feedback is to let a person know the results of his or her behavior. Feedback is a fair and clear discussion, and it is used to correct negative behavior and reinforce or support positive behavior. Giving feedback helps your employee develop the more objective self-understanding necessary for positive action and personal growth.

You have to do some preparation to give feedback: You must be ready to describe the problem and talk about its importance. You want to have some ideas about how to actively involve the employee in the solution to this problem. Your tone is supportive and collaborative.

You have several objectives when you give feedback:

- You want to bring about behavior change.
- You want to impress upon the employee the seriousness of the situation.
- You want to elicit from the employee whatever information he or she might have.
- You want the employee to understand clearly the nature of your concerns and your commitment to resolving those concerns.
- You want to arrive at solutions to the problem.

To achieve these objectives, you need to both give and receive feedback to achieve the greatest possible exchange of information and views.

For feedback to be effective, this one-to-one performance discussion must have the following characteristics:

- mutual trust (confidentiality, fairness, objectivity)
- recognition that the performance discussion is a mutual exploration to arrive at a solution
- two-way listening
- supportive behavior on your part to make it easier for the employee to talk

In this type of an environment, feedback on any of the following behaviors can lead to remedies for performance problems:

- discrepancies between statements and actions, verbal and nonverbal expressions

- distortions of self, job responsibilities, relationships
- evasion or avoidance of issues
- impact on others
- perceptions of strengths, weaknesses, and resources
- adequacy or functionality of coping behaviors
- defensive or manipulative behaviors
- appropriateness of responses to stress or conflict

The following guidelines will help you to keep your feedback constructive. Remember, this is an opportunity for development.

Limit your emotional response. In his book, *The One Minute Manager,* management consultant Ken Blanchard cautions against dwelling on disappointment over someone's less-than-satisfactory performance. He recommends that you state your feelings clearly, just once and without discussion, and then focus on solutions. It is important to convey how you feel about what happened, but after you have made your point, move on. Nothing is gained by beating the employee over the head again and again with your disappointment.

Focus on a person's behavior, not his self-esteem. For example, say, "You've been late getting back from lunch three times this week," rather than, "You like to socialize too much."

Be descriptive, not judgmental. Report your observations of what has occurred and let the employee use the feedback as he or she sees fit. When you use judgmental language, you are labeling the employee as good or bad, right or wrong. This puts anyone on the defensive and blocks communication. For example: "I have noticed . . ." or "I am concerned about . . ." is descriptive, but "You didn't finish the report . . ." or "Your trouble is . . ." is judgmental.

Be specific, particularly about time and events. "Last week's report contains two errors" is a fact that can be dealt with; "You didn't seem to care about the work" is too vague to be useful.

Deal with the effect and do not try to imply what caused it. Talk about what you know, not what you suspect. For example: "Several letters had to be retyped" is more helpful than "You must have been too upset by something to concentrate."

Use qualifiers and avoid all-or-nothing language. "Sometimes you rush through your work and quality suffers" is going to move the discussion forward; "You never take the time . . ." or "You always rush . . ." will set up barriers between you and the other person.

Give feedback as soon as it's appropriate. Bringing up something that happened three months ago is probably too late; starting a discussion on the warehouse floor while the rest of the shift is listening is too soon.

Focus on the controllable and changeable. Wish lists like this do not help: "If you just had not done that . . ." and "With fewer health problems, . . ." Find the workable options and don't dwell on the factors that are beyond control.

Do not demand change. You can't force someone to do something he doesn't want to do, so
don't try. "I've told you what is wrong, so
change" will yield temporary results only. People don't change for you, they change for themselves. "This is what will happen if this
disruptive behavior continues . . ." places the
responsibility for deciding to change where it
needs to be.

Share ideas and information, not advice. Help
your employee make the right decisions by
providing information and sparking new ideas.
You will evoke more lasting change by saying
something like, "It may be helpful to try . . ."
or "Have you thought about . . ." than if you
say, "What you ought to do is. . . ."

Share something of yourself. No one likes to talk
to someone who has all the answers, has never
been confused, or has never struggled with similar problems. Your relationships with your employees will be richer and more productive
(meaning that you will really listen to each other
more), if you let others know that you have feelings, concerns, and vulnerabilities. Don't
overdo it, though; save your lectures and war
stories for another audience.

Check for understanding. Even well-intentioned
feedback can be misinterpreted. Summarize frequently, bring each point to a conclusion as it
comes up, stay on a subject until you've both
spoken your mind, and rephrase what the other
says to be sure the meaning is clear. For example: "It sounds as if you want me to think of
new ways to report our quality checks" and

"Are we both singing out of the same songbook?
As I understand it, we agree that. . . ."

SUGGESTIONS FOR ASKING FOR FEEDBACK

Performance discussions are not only a fair and efficient means of dealing with many of the issues that block improved productivity, but they are also an excellent opportunity to uncover new ideas, potential problems, and valuable reactions to the plans and programs you have underway.

Also, asking for feedback balances the tone of the discussion with your employee. Rather than just "talking at" your employee, you can make an explicit request of him or her to help you think through some aspects of working together. This adds substance to your commitment to be collaborative.

Keep in mind that giving feedback to you, the boss, will not come easily to every one of your employees. Some will be intimidated ("Gee, he's the boss. What can I say to him that will help? I don't want to sound like an idiot."). Some will be confused ("What does this guy want from me?" or "He's the boss—why is he asking *me*?"). Some will not know what to do with the opportunity ("Oh boy, this is my chance to blow off steam and tell him everything that I think ought to be changed in the data processing department.").

Here are some techniques that will increase both the quantity and quality of the feedback you receive:

Ask more open-ended questions and fewer closed-ended questions. Questions beginning with words like "do," "will," "would," "is," "are" tend to invite yes or no responses. For example: "Is that clear?" and "You know whom to call, don't you?" Open-ended questions begin with the words "who," "what," "when," "where," "why," and "how." Questions beginning with these six words tend to bring out more information because they are difficult to answer with a simple yes or no. Compare the following examples with the closed-ended questions just mentioned: "What questions do you have?" "How can I clarify that?" "Who will you call for the information?"

Ask "suppose" questions.   Suppose questions require the listener to place himself in someone else's position and respond as he or she thinks that other person should. For example, "If it were your problem, how would you handle it?" is a typical suppose question.

Echo.   Echoing is the repetition of a speaker's words. Followed by a pause, it encourages the speaker to elaborate on that point. For example, "You feel I'm not being fair?"

Reassure.   Reassurance is letting the speaker know that you empathize with him or her because you have been in a similar situation or had similar feelings yourself. For example: "The end of the year is rough. I remember how uptight I always felt until all audit reports were finished."

Reflect.   Reflection is a neutral observation of the feelings you see in another person. "You seem very frustrated about this" is a reflective statement.

Listen. People say more, and they say it better, when they believe someone is really listening to them. Good listeners are called *active listeners* because they are actively not passively involved in the discussion. They are focused on the ideas the speaker is expressing and are choosing to filter out internal and external distractions.

The following suggestions will help you to become a more active listener:

a. Be attentive to the other person, psychologically and physically.
b. Paraphrase key ideas to clarify and confirm meaning.
c. Ask questions, but don't interview.
d. Keep the discussion on track, focused, and moving.
e. Summarize the major points you think you hear.

COMMUNICATING ABOUT GOOD PERFORMANCE

Telling someone he or she is doing a good job sounds easy. This is not true. We are not practiced in giving praise. Most of us have grown up hearing a lot about what we are doing wrong and very little about what we are doing right. Is it any wonder that "no feedback is good feedback" for most of us? The praise and recognition we do receive is often too little and too late, and it usually depends on an award or contest or other competitive event. Since there is only one winner, are all the rest of us losers? Of course not.

Actually, the fact that praise is so uncommon makes it that much more powerful when it is used to reward good performance. Imagine yourself on the receiving end of the following comments:

"You're doing a great job . . . and I want to let you know we appreciate your contributions to this."

"Thank you."

"Thank you for . . . (coming up with that solution; staying late to finish; staying with the job until it was finished, even though it was something you didn't like to do; caring enough to do it right; being here on time every day)."

"What you do is very important to the next group down the line. Because you are such a stickler for quality, they have an easier time with their part and the whole operation runs more smoothly."

"Your suggestion has saved us time and money. Thank you—and here is . . . (a bonus, complimentary tickets, a certificate, a round of applause) to let you know that we really appreciate your help in making this a better place to work."

Get the idea? It's less important what you say than how you say it. If you say it at all—and you are sincere—you will unleash the tremendous power of positive reinforcement.

Remember: You get more of the behavior that you recognize and reward. If you want more workers to come in early, start complimenting the early arrivals, keep track of arrival times, or make free donuts available. If you want to improve productivity, let everyone know how you are measuring productivity, publicize the results, and spotlight new ideas and outstanding efforts that contribute to the goal. This is basic: Your people want to do well and be recognized for their efforts because it makes them feel good about themselves. Recognize and reward good performance to get more of it.

There are many ways to acknowledge good performance. Ideally, your recognition or reward will feel right for the person and circumstance. An encouraging word is probably appropriate for work in progress, whereas a formal public acknowledgment would be suitable for milestone results. As we discussed in the chapter about influencing, different people are motivated by different rewards.

Two obvious ways to reward a person is to give him or her a promotion and/or increased compensation. But these can be used only infrequently. Some other ways to acknowledge good performance are the following:

- awards (cash, trophy, certificate, travel)
- recognition in the company newspaper or on the plant bulletin board
- increased responsibility (special projects, committee or task force leadership, United Way chairmanship)
- special training
- memberships in professional or trade associations as the company representative

Can you overpraise? Yes. Use common sense. If everything is treated as a major accomplishment, or if everything is given equal acknowledgment, workers will not be motivated to push themselves to get big results for big recognition. Give them a taste of positive rewards at whatever level they've earned them—even if it is simply for showing up for work and doing their job—and they will begin to work hard for more of it. For most people, positive feedback is its own reward because it reinforces their self-esteem.

Here are a few ways to remind ourselves to recognize and reward our employees' good performance:

- Make a review of key productivity measurements a part of your routine; then, generously administer compliments and other positive feedback.
- Give your employees opportunities to talk to you casually; they will tell you what they are proud of! Purposely stand around during a break, walk around the plant, ask questions of an operator, share a story of your weekend in a relaxed manner; when you do, you signal to your employees that this is a good time to approach you.
- Start a suggestion box. It's corny, but it's a recognized communication channel that is nonthreatening.
- Watch for individual contributions to the corporate goals. If new account development is a priority, make a big deal out of it when your workers respond with ideas and actions. The "Employee of the Week" (or Month) programs are popular because they work.

- Publicize progress toward the group's goals. Put your output chart up in the employee lunchroom. Help your people feel good every day about doing a good job.

Don't underestimate the power of praise. Because it encourages people to want to do well, it is more powerful than a reprimand. It is also easier to administer. As you will see in the next section, correcting behavior requires an unceasing effort to push people toward what you want them to do and pull them back from what you don't want them to do.

COMMUNICATING ABOUT POOR PERFORMANCE

It is natural to avoid conversations about poor performance because they are as uncomfortable to give as to receive. We don't like being judged, and we don't like feeling as if we are judging someone else.

It is also natural to dislike discussions about performance because this puts us in conflict with one of our favorite myths: Everything and everyone is doing well. It's human nature to give people the benefit of the doubt, excuse them, and hope the problem will take care of itself. "We've got the best people in the business," you tell yourself. "If they can't get their work done, there must be a good reason." Realistically, you probably have your share of outstanding performers, mediocre performers, well-intentioned incompetents, and all the rest.

Communicating about poor performance is also risky for working relationships. You may often be put in situations in which you must take corrective action when you are not completely prepared. Are your instincts always right, or does your unintentional bias, prejudice, lack of clear standards, lack of information about the job or the work sometimes yield an unfair evaluation of performance? If you are wrong or handle the discussion badly, you have put a chip on the shoulder of someone with whom you will have to work again.

But significant performance problems inevitably creep into the work flow. The difficulty is not in identifying a performance problem, but in deciding what to do about it. Consider Doug's problem with Tricia during a recent performance discussion:

Doug: "What's going on, Tricia? I know you understand the plan for our department. You know what our objectives are, and you know we've gone to a lot of trouble to reorganize the shift schedule to accommodate everyone's needs. Up until last week, your production was good—I think you even had a shot at the Hawaii trip, didn't you?"

Tricia: "I suppose so. I was really excited about that."

Doug: "Was? Why not now? Your production has dropped back to where it was before."

Tricia: "I know. I can't really explain it, but . . ."

Doug: "Doggone it, Tricia—just do it. I'm going to be watching your numbers, and they better be up again by next week."

In the exchange above, Doug squandered a good opportunity to learn more about how the new process was working. He believed he had done his job, and it was time for the employees to do theirs. But new plans, new ways of organizing, incentives, and control measures don't get the work done. That comes out of one-to-one discussions about performance. Remember that every performance discussion is an opportunity for your workers to develop their skills. They learn the most on the job, and you are their best teacher.

GETTING STARTED

Let's apply some communication skills to approach some sample performance problems.

Step 1. Ask yourself whether there really is a performance problem here. Or, is this a communication problem? Before you say anything to anyone about what you perceive as a performance problem, stop and think about what you expected to occur and what actually happened. Consider the following:

a. Were mutual performance expectations clearly understood?
   (1) What precisely was your understanding?
   (2) Specifically how was performance to be measured? Are you still satisfied that the measurement was fair?

     (3) Could this possibly be a communication problem? If so, the problem of poor performance remains, but you will need to handle it differently.

  b. What was the actual performance?

     (1) Job performance that can be easily observed and measured can be described in terms of action, result, and time.

     Example: *Henrietta made presentations to 15 clubs and sold $100,000 worth of new orders in the past two weeks.*

     (2) Job performance that is not easily observed and seldom documented is more difficult to evaluate objectively. Rather than relying on your impressions, establish specific milestones of progress within specific time frames.

     Example: *Warren finished the research on one-half of the cities in Michigan by the end of the week.*

     (3) Job performance that is unpredictable or otherwise hard to measure must be evaluated in terms of observable behaviors, however infrequent, and their consequential results. Then, a baseline for behaviors or outcomes can be established by averaging whatever figures are meaningful over a longer time period.

     Example: *Thelma's public relations efforts yielded a 15 percent increased awareness of the smog problem based on the increase in the number of calls to the hot line. The increase in the number of articles longer than 250 words run in the newspapers has also been significant, al-*

> *though the impact is more difficult to measure.*

c. What is the difference between the actual and expected performance? Is there a performance gap?

   (1) What exactly is the performance problem? (How long has it been a problem? When and where does it or does it NOT occur? How often does it occur?)

   (2) Is the performance gap important? (What impact does the incorrect performance have on the quality, quantity, and cost of the product or service? What impact does the wrong performance have on the corporate image, safety, or other employees?)

   (3) Has this employee ever done this correctly? (If so, when? If not, has anyone ever performed this correctly? How were the circumstances similar or different?)

   (4) How will you know when the problem is solved? What will be different?

Step 2. *Ask yourself whether this is a "can't do" or "won't do" problem?* Answering this question will help you understand where the difficulty originates and to select the best approach to solving the problem. Most frequently, any one or a combination of the following four factors could be involved:

Aptitude. A person with poor manual dexterity will never be able to excel at a task like typing or repairing delicate electronic equipment. Given a supportive and patient supervisor, however, he or she could possibly be brought up to an acceptable level of performance.

Ability.   Some persons have sufficient aptitude for a given task but their abilities have not been developed to take full advantage of their aptitude.

Interest.   You have probably dealt with persons who had the aptitude and ability to perform well but who, for whatever reason, simply lacked interest and performed at a level well below their capabilities.

Attitude.   A person's attitude affects his or her performance. If a person resents authority, he or she will not respond well to directives, will probably do only what must be done and, in general, will require closer supervision than you would like.

A *can't do* performance problem exists when an employee cannot for some reason perform as expected. The person does not lack willingness, but lacks aptitude or ability or both.

A *won't do* performance problem exists when an employee appears to have all the resources and capabilities for performing the job or activity properly, but is not doing so. A won't do problem is an interest and attitude problem.

Determining whether an employee has a can't do or won't do performance problem will not make communicating about it easier, but you will at least be able to focus your discussion on potential remedies instead of excuses and defensiveness.

Step 3. *Coach or counsel your employee.* Whether your approach is coaching or counseling, pick the right time to discuss the performance problem. You may need to address the problem immediately if there is a possibility of injury, high cost, or the creation of an even larger problem. On the other hand, you may want to wait until after emotions have cooled.

The performance discussion may be as casual as a few moments together in the hallway or at the water cooler, or it may be a closed-door conversation lasting a half-hour or longer. Pick a time and place for your discussion that will minimize distractions and anything else that could confuse the issues.

Coaching conversations are effective with can't do performance problems—those relating to aptitude and ability. They are generally developmental in tone and intended to train and reinforce the behavior of the employee. They are usually not held in response to a particular incident of poor performance.

The manager may initiate a coaching conversation to discuss broadening an employee's responsibilities or to address minor problems of changes that can be resolved with instructions or new information. Coaching conversations are also used to reinforce good performance by giving the employee more frequent positive feedback about his behavior or results.

Coaching conversations tend to look far into the future: "We're going to have to get started on your development as a lead pressman, Bob. You know that Frank is going to be retiring soon and we have two new presses on the way, so we've got to figure out a plan to get you up to speed."

The employee may initiate a coaching conversation to get additional information ("What do you think of what I did, boss?" or "How did that work?") or to give feedback to you ("Our plan didn't work quite the way we intended . . .").

Counseling conversations focus on the won't do problems of attitude and interest. They are usually intended to help the employee modify his behavior in order to achieve the results desired by the manager. They generally are intended to improve the employee's performance in a specific area. Counseling is used most often to address minor performance problems that can be resolved by communicating or clarifying consequences or incentives.

When counseling an employee, you will want to

- describe the problem as neutrally and objectively as possible by using descriptive statements.
- indicate the impact of the problem on you, the employee's co-workers, and anyone else who is affected.
- probe for details from the employee's viewpoint. The employee may have information you do not have. Use open-ended questions to bring that information out and LISTEN! LISTEN! LISTEN!
- discuss solutions to the problem. What can you and/or the employee do to correct the situation?
- agree on an action plan and decide when you and the employee will sit down again to review results.

Coaching and counseling conversations work because they are

- short, usually between three and ten minutes.
- informal, as name suggests, they are conversational in tone.

- typically unscheduled or arranged only shortly in advance.

Coaching and counseling conversations are private and personal. Although some small group team meetings could be considered coaching conversations, most coaching and counseling conversations are held in a private, one-to-one setting. No documentation is required, although it may be useful to jot a few notes down to use in the next formal performance review.

WHEN PERFORMANCE DOESN'T IMPROVE

In spite of your best efforts, the performance of some of your employees may not improve. Eventually, you will have to decide to escalate the performance issue in order to resolve it, or ignore it. Your options include a process of progressive disciplinary actions leading up to termination.

In the workplace, disciplinary actions mean development, not punishment. It is an extension of the values we expressed earlier:

- We are partners in this business enterprise.
- Each of us have our jobs to do.
- We are committed to each other's success.
- When one of us chooses not to do his or her job, the rest of us have to choose a new partner with whom we can work.

Escalating your response to include disciplinary actions or termination is a serious decision. You and the company have an investment in the employee, and your actions from here forward put that investment at risk.

Strong disciplinary action—up to and including discharge—on a first offense may be invoked when the employee commits a very serious violation of the company's rules. There is universal agreement that certain behaviors are totally unacceptable, such as stealing, destruction of company property, and deliberate actions that put safety at risk.

Less serious infractions, such as chronic lateness, require a progressive disciplinary response. These are problems too serious to ignore, yet are not so serious that the company has to cut its losses and terminate its investment in the employee. As manager, you must establish a specific incident or pattern of unacceptable performance before you begin a disciplinary response. Poor quality work resulting in a client complaint, for example, may happen once or many times before disciplinary action is triggered; as long as you are providing the employee with clear and consistent feedback, you can keep your options open.

Improving Performance: A Progressive Approach

The most successful and fair approach to improving an employee's performance is a process of

1. communicating progressively more directive verbal and written messages ("You WILL finish the assignment in the warehouse by Tuesday . . ."), and

    2. administering progressively more negative consequences for noncompliance.

In other words, you "turn up the heat" until you get the employee's attention and cause him to choose to improve his performance. By telling him what the negative consequence of poor performance is in advance, you give him every reasonable opportunity to decide to do his job in the way that meets your expectations. When you do this, you are strongly influencing his development of his career choices, self-control, and decision-making skills. If he implicitly or explicitly decides he does or does not want to work for you, his performance will reflect his choice.

A progressive disciplinary approach recognizes that you cannot force people to do something they don't want to do; nor can you afford to tolerate poor performance indefinitely. You may not be able to control him but you can control the quantity and quality of work standards that the company finds acceptable. This approach recognizes that even though the employee may be content to drift with below-par work, you have no such luxury. You must fire such a person who has mentally quit his or her job and get someone in who can do the job right. The sooner you get a poor performer replaced, the better for everyone, including the employee.

Most of us will go to extraordinary lengths to rationalize employee behavior so that we can avoid this uncomfortable and difficult process. We avoid it as long as possible because

- we hope the problem will go away.
- we know that if we start it, we have to finish it, even when we can't "fix" the situation.

- we are afraid that the whole thing will somehow blow up in our faces.
- we just aren't sure what to do.

Except for the most serious offenses that require immediate termination, offering employees progressively more serious consequences to their actions is a preferred strategy. A progressive approach ensures clear communication about the issue, ample opportunities to discuss it, and gives the employee plenty of time to change his or her behavior.

Keep in mind that you are simply providing feedback to the employee about his actions. You are setting the standards, and communicating what is considered acceptable and not acceptable performance. Based on the feedback he gets from you, he makes his choices: Does he do things differently next time, or doesn't he? Because the process escalates only when he fails to change and make the necessary improvements, he can stop the negative consequences at any time by choosing to comply.

When you have a performance problem, your company's version of a progressive approach to discipline should include most of the following six steps:

Step 1. An informal discussion about the difference between performance expectations and actual results

Step 2. An oral warning that performance has not improved

Step 3. A written warning that becomes a part of the permanent personnel file

Step 4. A second oral or written warning that becomes a part of the permanent personnel file

Step 5. Suspension

Step 6. Discharge

Here's what happens at each step:

Step 1. The informal discussion. The purpose of step 1 is to communicate clearly about the gap between expected and actual performance. This puts the employee on notice that there is a problem and presents the corrective action he must take. Here is your opportunity to clear up any communication problems that may exist. Your goals are to explain the rule violated and why it exists, to uncover and resolve any problems the employee may have in meeting the rule, and to express confidence in the employee's avoiding similar situations in the future. At the conclusion of this discussion, the employee should have no doubt as to what is expected of him.

The informal discussion is entirely off the record; make no notes other than those you will need to follow up on the employee's progress in a few weeks, and do not put anything into his personnel file.

Common problems that can be solved at this first step of the process are excessive lateness, absenteeism, prolonged breaks, low productivity, and inferior quality of work. Those and similar problems frequently can be resolved early. The key to change is an effective discussion emphasizing problem solving.

Let's use Ruth and her conversation with her supervisor as an example of how the informal discussion works. Ruth is a customer service representative who has been late three times and absent twice (including yesterday) within the past month. Ruth has been with the company for eight months and, until now, has presented no other problems; so, an informal discussion seems appropriate.

The supervisor calls Ruth into her office and begins by saying:

"Good morning, Ruth. Please sit down. I want to talk to you informally about your attendance. I'm concerned that we may have a problem, and it's beginning to affect your performance and the performance of others."

Ruth: "Look, I know I've been late a couple times, but I'm not the only one . . "

Supervisor: "Well, let's see. My records indicate you've been late three times and absent twice in the last month. Does that sound right?"

Ruth: "Yes, I guess so. But I didn't mean to be late, and one of those absences just couldn't be helped!"

Supervisor: "Ruth, there's no need to get defensive. I'm just trying to solve our problem."

Ruth: "Just how much trouble am I in?"

Supervisor: "That's going to be up to you. I want to review a couple of points with you and make our position clear, okay?"

Ruth: "Sure. Go ahead."

Supervisor: "To start with, do you understand that to give our customers proper service, you must be available? As you know, you are always working on estimates and schedules with our customers in the eastern region. No one else can fill in for you on short notice. Maybe we should be organized differently, but we aren't right now. They start calling us at the crack of dawn, and if you are not here to help them, they don't get the answers they need. You're an important part of our team, and you are badly missed when you aren't here."

Ruth: "I understand that, of course."

Supervisor: "I'm sure you do—or did. Up until a month ago, I could always rely on you to be here on time, every day. What's going on? Are you unhappy with your job?"

Ruth: "No—I love my job. The real problem is my husband's working hours. Until about six weeks ago, he worked the 4 P.M. to midnight shift, which means he was home during the day to look after the twins. His company changed his hours to day shift and now he has to leave at 7:00 A.M. So, if the nursery school bus is late or Jimmy is sick, my husband isn't there to help."

Supervisor: "This sounds like a difficult situation for you."

Ruth: "It is. Even on the good days, I can just barely make it here on time. It sure makes for a hectic morning."

Supervisor: "I can imagine. What do you plan to do?"

At this point, Ruth became very distressed and admitted she had no solutions. It was clear to her supervisor that Ruth had unrealistic hopes that the situation would "just work itself out, somehow, someway."

Supervisor: "Ruth, I can't decide for you how to solve this problem, but I want to try to help. You're a valued member of our team here, and I need you to be here on time and in the proper frame of mind to help our customers. What's keeping you from solving this problem?"

Ruth: "Time. I think I need to find a way to handle the twins differently in the morning, and that means talking to the day care center, other parents, maybe even my neighbors. I may even have to switch day care centers."

Supervisor: "How much time do you need?"

Ruth: "Well, a few hours. It's impossible to do on the phone . . ."

Supervisor: "If I give you next Tuesday and Thursday afternoons off, would that give you enough time to find a solution?"

> *Ruth:* "Gosh, I'll make it work. That would be great . . ."

Ruth returned with her problem solved. Her supervisor only vaguely knows the details—Ruth now has some sort of an arrangement with a neighbor and a parent's car pool—but she doesn't even need to know that much. Ruth's supervisor is satisfied to know that this valued employee has not been late once in three weeks and has returned to her previous level of effectiveness with the customers in the eastern region.

Sound easy? Well, the supervisor needed to apply many of the skills we've discussed. For example:

a . She described the specific actions and behaviors that were becoming problems.

b . She explained how Ruth's actions and behaviors were affecting performance and reviewed why it was important that Ruth meet performance expectations.

c . She encouraged Ruth to find her own solutions and supported her efforts to do so. Throughout the discussion, Ruth continued to "own" her problem and her responsibility, and the supervisor was careful not to get so involved with finding the solution that it would no longer belong to Ruth. (After all, Ruth will have to make her solution work.)

d . She avoided generalizations and personal attacks.

e . She listened carefully, alternately echoing and leading Ruth's comments as they thought through the problem together.

f . She asked open-ended questions that would elicit information.

g . She reviewed and asserted her expectations for Ruth's performance.

h . She expressed her understanding and sympathy of Ruth's feelings and problems.

i . She was encouraging and supportive.

Sometimes the informal discussion does not bring about sufficient improvement. Or, you may need a more formal discussion sooner. In either case, use the oral warning.

Step 2. The oral warning. Step 2 is the first formal, documented step in a progressive disciplinary process. You will want to

- describe the infraction and its impact,
- review previous discussions you might have had, especially if they were during the past year,
- ask the employee to explain the situation from his/her viewpoint,
- ask how he/she will avoid recurrences,
- agree on actions you and/or the employee will take,

- let the employee know what disciplinary action you are now taking,
- inform the employee that you will prepare a memo on this discussion which will be held in the files for one year,
- advise the employee that a recurrence might result in further disciplinary action,
- express confidence in the employee's ability to resolve the situation,
- set a specific date for a follow-up discussion to review progress.

Following the discussion, you should prepare a file memo summarizing each of the above steps. If, at the end of one year no further action has been required, the memo should be given to the employee. This helps to convince the employee that the matter is closed and that he/she now has a "clean slate." It also gives you a formal opportunity to recognize the employee's successful efforts.

To illustrate, let's consider the case of John, a public utility repairman. Basically, John's job is to respond to customer complaints about leaks, discover the source of the leak, and make necessary repairs. The department's experience has shown that about 2% of a repairman's calls result in "call-backs"; in other words, the customer calls again because the leak has not been eliminated. John seems to be having more than his share of problems.

John's supervisor calls him into his office and says:

"John, I want to talk to you again about the number of call-backs you've been getting. We've talked informally about this issue twice in the last three months and it's still a problem."

John: "What's wrong now?"

Supervisor: "Your call-back rate is running about 4½ percent—more than twice our standard. As you know, call-backs are expensive and bad for customer relations."

John: "I've just been having bad luck."

Supervisor: "I don't think it's a matter of luck, John. The call-back reports indicate a lack of care in doing the repairs. Last week, for example, you repaired a pinhole in a lead-in pipe by plugging the hole, but you neglected to wrap the pipe in safety tape. As a result, the plug worked loose and we got a call-back. Actions like these really count for a good part of the 4½ percent. Aside from bad luck, what other reasons do you think might account for your high call-back rate?"

John: "I don't know. I just think you're out to get me. You're always calling me on the carpet. The other guys make mistakes too, you know!"

Supervisor: "I realize that. I made mistakes when I was a repairman, too. John, we have to face it. You're having more problems than you should and I'd like some ideas from you on how these incidents can be avoided . . . (Pause)"

John: "I don't know."

Supervisor: "Let me first suggest that you review the procedures manual. It might also help if I put you in the brush-up program."

John: "Those are good ideas, but they won't help. I know the work."

Supervisor: "Maybe it won't solve all the problems, John, but these are at least steps in the right direction. Do you have any other ideas?"

John blurted out that what he really needed was a good night's sleep. "Tell me what you mean, John," said the manager. John said he had not been sleeping well because of personal problems, and this made it hard for him to concentrate day after day.

Supervisor: "John, I don't know how to solve your problems, but this gives me an idea as to how we can solve ours. Would it help to talk to the company's employee assistance counselor?"

John: "The what?"

Supervisor: "The employee assistance counselor. He's trained to help you get through whatever problems you're having that keep you from doing your best work. You know—financial, emotional, drinking . . ."

John: "I guess I'm an old-fashioned guy like my Dad. I was raised to keep my problems to myself, so I just figured that I would eventually get these worked out."

Supervisor: "Old-fashioned or not, it sounds as if you could use some help . . . should I set it up?"

John: "Gee, I don't know . . ."

Supervisor: "Let me put it this way: I think you need some help. I'm very serious about this. If your work doesn't improve, you leave me no choice but to take further disciplinary action. We've had informal talks in the past, but this discussion is an oral warning. I will have to speak to the superintendent as well as write a memo documenting our discussion and place it in your personnel file. This will stay in your record for the next year. If you come up to standard and remain there, I'll be very happy to remove it from the file."

John: "You're not being fair!"

Supervisor: "What's there to be fair about? You know you have been expected to change, yet you have chosen not to seek help. Now I am offering it to you again, and I'll keep getting tougher on you until you take it. Now which will it be: the EAP counselor or the retraining, or both?"

John soon received the help he needed. His supervisor was satisfied that whatever was distracting him was resolved to the extent that his performance returned to normal.

The oral warning differed from the informal discussion in two important ways:

a . The discussion was no longer just between supervisor and employee. The supervisor's superior had been notified that a problem existed.

b. Following the oral warning, the supervisor placed a memo in the employee's file which summarizes the discussion.

Step. 3. The written warning.   Most disciplinary situations can be handled as informal discussions or oral warnings. The written warning, however, differs significantly in the following respects:

a. The discussion may be conducted by or in the presence of your superior to further emphasize the gravity of this step.

b. Another memo is placed in the employee's file. This time, however, it will remain there for an indefinite period of time.

c. A letter of warning is also placed in the employee's file, which fully describes the problem, and attempts to resolve it. The letter to file also contains the employee's response, the agreed-upon plan for corrective action, the possible consequences for further poor performance, and a future date to review progress. The letter is read and given to the employee as part of the disciplinary discussion. Many organizations request the employee to sign the file copy as evidence that the employee received and understood it.

Step. 4. A second oral or written warning that becomes a part of the permanent personnel file.   Some organizations, particularly those that must be in strict compliance with personnel quotas to maintain their government contracts, may feel the need to take this extra step to document their efforts to be fair and reasonable with an offending employee.

Step. 5. Suspension. Some organizations do not use suspension as part of their progressive discipline process. It should be considered for the following reasons:

a . None of the preceding steps has imposed an economic penalty. Until that happens, some employees may not take the progressive discipline process seriously. The added pressures caused by a loss of income may finally cause a change in the employee's behavior.

b . If a third party is to review an eventual discharge, the fact that no improvement took place after one or a series of suspensions will weigh heavily in your favor.

Most organizations that use suspension as part of the process approach it in one of two ways: a severe (three- or five-day) suspension following an unsuccessful written warning OR a series of suspensions—generally a one-day followed by a three-day and, finally a five-day suspension. The discussion procedures to be used at the time of suspension are the same as for the oral warning, and documentation is the same as that for the written warning.

Step. 6. Discharge. If you have followed the preceding steps and the employee's behavior has not changed, you are left with no choice but corporate capital punishment—discharge.

By now, you have probably resigned yourself to losing this employee, but others may disagree. You can avoid being reversed and having the employee reinstated by being aware of what a third party typically looks for when reviewing a discharge. When hearing a dismissal appeal, third parties basically want to be assured that you took every precaution to deal fairly with the employee. Here are some major factors they take into consideration:

a. *Forewarning.* Can you demonstrate that the employee has been informed of your expectations, his or her performance, and any alleged performance gap? You don't have to forewarn employees that theft, willful destruction of property, drinking on the job, and other major violations of the rules are grounds for immediate dismissal. But standards regarding lateness, absences, quality of work, and so on, need to be communicated because expectations vary so much from one organization to another.

b. *Probable consequences.* Employees must be informed of what may happen if their behavior continues. The choice is then theirs.

c. *Reasonable rules.* Can you demonstrate that the rule fills a business need? Does it apply to all employees in the work unit?

d. *Documentation.* Is it complete? Was it done at the time of your discussion?

e. *Penalties.* Are they realistic or excessive? Were they imposed soon after the occurrence or at a later date?

f . *Right to appeal.* Did the employee have access to higher levels of management to explain his or her views?

Progressive disciplinary action is the end of your performance management system. Think the employee's performance problem through thoroughly. Have you done everything possible to identify and develop this employee's strengths? Have you been sincere and reasonable in finding a solution? Will your forthcoming actions be regarded as fair, or will they be a surprise and appear arbitrary? Are you prepared to lose this employee? Careful consideration of certain issues can put you in a more comfortable and confident position when you take that initial disciplinary action or when a subsequent action seems necessary. Some of the more important considerations are:

Timing. How much time has elapsed since the last infraction and discussion? The shorter the time span, the greater the latitude we have in moving the incident from an oral warning to a written warning. Generally, if one year has elapsed since the last infraction, you must begin the process all over again.

General performance pattern. Is this infraction part of a pattern of marginal or poor performance? Is it the first instance? If the problem is recurring and part of a pattern, stronger disciplinary action may be appropriate. On the other hand, if this behavior is unusual for this employee, you will probably want to refrain from strong action.

Clear understanding of expectations. Are you certain that this employee is aware of the company's standards? Many supervisors, as part of their new employee orientation, make a point of sitting down with new employees and reviewing the standards and policies relating to absences, breaks, and so on. This kind of discussion also offers an ideal opportunity to communicate the reasons for the expectations.

Precedent.   How have similar infractions been handled in the past? Unless you can demonstrate that this situation or this employee is different, you must respond just as you would have in the past. This does not mean, however, that after a traditional response has been established, it cannot be changed. To bring about change requires you to do two things: First, you should communicate the new rule to all employees; second, you should allow a reasonable time for the persons involved to adjust their behavior. During this transition phase, you should have an informal performance discussion when an infraction occurs.

Effect on co-workers.   What is the effect of this employee's behavior on other members of the work force? Your action (or inaction) almost always has an effect on other employees. Are people entitled to longer breaks, for example, when they work faster than anyone else? Are you making yourself vulnerable to possible charges of favoritism? Do your responses to problems build or tear down morale.

Special circumstances.   What unique factors contributed to this situation? Personal pressures from home, changing health conditions, or a suddenly heavier workload may cause performance to slide temporarily; an employee in this position needs compassion and extra help, not more pressure.

Seniority. Seniority usually matters. The greater an employee's seniority, the more reluctant a third party will be to uphold severe disciplinary action, except in the most serious situations. It is reasonable, for example, to suspend a senior person when a relatively new employee would be discharged for the same infraction.

Defense. If an employee appeals your action, will you be able to adequately defend yourself? Do you have evidence, witnesses, or documentation that demonstrates that your action was reasonable?

How would you handle the special considerations in the following circumstances?

1. In reviewing the monthly materials waste report, you discover that Karen has waste that is almost twice that of the group average. She has already received an oral warning for this problem. What options do you have if the oral warning was given:
   a. 14 months ago?
   b. last month?
   c. 11 months ago?

(Your options will be customarily limited by applying the one-year rule. If at least a year has elapsed since the oral warning, it is assumed that the employee has [or had] learned her lesson and is entitled to start the disciplinary process over again with another oral warning. If the last warning was within the year, you can move to a written warning. Obviously, 11 months is borderline and you have to consider general performance during that period and any special circumstances that might now exist in the current situation.)

2. Greg and Paul were found sleeping in a company truck by a district supervisor. Greg has been with the company 18 years and has had a very good record. Paul, however, has been in trouble before. During his two years with the company, you have had talks with him about some of his practices, one of which led to a written warning about three months ago. Both Greg and Paul are fully aware that sleeping on duty is considered a major infraction and could result in discharge. You have decided to discharge Paul.

   a. Can you discharge Paul and not Greg?
   b. What difference does Greg's seniority make?
   c. Considering the seriousness of the infraction, what disciplinary action would seem appropriate in your dealings with Greg?

(You can expect to receive some pressure to treat both men equally. But remember, your objective is to be fair, and equal treatment is not always the same as fair treatment. Whenever you decide to treat one employee differently from another, you take on the additional burden of possibly having to defend the difference in treatment. In this case, there are substantial reasons for treating Greg and Paul differently. Unlike Paul, Greg has a long history with the company and he also has a very good record. Greg's co-workers would probably see discharging him as overkill. As Greg's manager, however, you cannot avoid taking some quite severe disciplinary action with him. Suspending Greg for one or two weeks [without pay] would seem to be an appropriate response.)

3. For several years, it has been the practice of machine operators in your area to punch out about ten minutes before the end of their shift. The former plant manager knew the employees who did this, but never said anything to them.

   This morning, however, you received a memo from the new plant manager saying the practice had to stop and, beginning immediately, anyone caught punching out early would be suspended for the following day. You immediately meet with the operators and read the memo to them. As a further precaution, you post the memo on the bulletin board. Ken, one of your longtime good employees, is out for the day and is not present at the meeting.

   The next day, in spite of the posted memo and your attempted intervention, Ken punches out early. You stop him as he is leaving early and tell him you have no choice but to suspend him for a day. Ken protests and says, "You know I have to leave early so I can see my wife before visiting hours at the hospital are over.

Besides, everyone's been doing this for years. Give me a break. I can't afford to lose a day's pay.'' You point out the memo on the bulletin board and tell Ken that's the way it has to be and there can be no exceptions. Ken says he'll go to the union.

  a. What do you think the union's position will be?

  b. What considerations do you think the union will present in arguing Ken's case?

  c. How do you think the situation should have been handled?

(The union will undoubtedly argue vigorously for Ken's defense, basing its case on the following points:

- timing [Ken had not personally been told of this change and lacked forewarning.]
- otherwise good general performance [Ken had a clear record and is considered one of the "better employees."]
- precedent [Punching out early had been an acceptable practice for many years.]
- special circumstances [Ken has a sick wife, and the visiting hour restrictions make it difficult for him to comply with the new rules.]
- seniority [Ken had been with the company too long to be treated in this shabby and arbitrary manner.]

As Ken's supervisor, you could have handled the situation more effectively by

- appealing to the plant manager about the advisability of suspension beginning immediately, i.e., "Surely this will have a negative effect on the other employees because it would be perceived as unfair; besides, how much harm has been done? What will it cost us to be lenient within the bounds of common sense?"

· insisting that the employees be given a week or two to adjust to the new rule before formal disciplinary action be taken

· recommending that infractions during the time of transition be handled by an informal discussion with the employee

· presenting to the plant manager Ken's situation and other cases in which a person may have a legitimate reason for leaving early; then, eliciting any ideas he or she has on how to handle these cases

· discussing the new rule with the plant manager before presenting the rule to the employees; by the time you present it, you should be able to support it, describe the reasons for it, and explain the length and purpose of the adjustment phase and what accommodations can be made for those who have special problems.)

4. Annabelle has been a superior payroll clerk in most respects for eight months. Your only problem with her occurred about four months ago when she failed to complete a quarterly report before she took a few days off, making it necessary for you to call in extra help. You talked to her upon her return, but didn't want to come down too hard because she is other-

wise very good at her job. In an off-handed way, you suggested she "try to finish all her work" before taking time off the next time. Last week, however, she mentioned on her way out the door for a three-day absence that she did not do the report again. You were upset that she left you and others to finish her work. Now that it has happened again, you are considering giving her an oral warning. During this morning's discussion, you discovered that Annabelle's interpretation of your last talk had been that you would like her to finish that report before she left if she had time, but it was not mandatory.

   a. Should you follow through on an oral warning? Why or why not?
   b. What points do you feel should be made in this discussion which were not covered in the previous talk?

(Given the informality of the first talk, Annabelle obviously did not feel forewarned. She may be faulted for poor judgment, but considering that you were unspecific about what you wanted done in your first discussion, her behavior was not unreasonable. Now is the time to make your expectations clear with another informal discussion. You will want to make the point that Annabelle must complete all her reports, including this one, before she takes time off. You may find it useful to point out that the reason for your insistence on this point is because of the negative consequences suffered by others when she does not complete her job.)

Supervisors who follow the progressive approach—in which each step becomes more serious—can feel secure about their actions. Their actions are fair and reasonable extensions of efforts to develop the employee to his or her full potential.

Disciplinary situations are never pleasant, but you can keep them in perspective if you remember that

- As with development activities, disciplinary activities communicate and reinforce the company's performance standards. Each employee chooses how to respond to these messages about performance.
- Your objective is not to punish, but to change behavior.
- You are not the aggressor. The employee's choices about his or her behavior create the need for discipline.
- Productive employees are demotivated when "problem employees" are ignored or tolerated.
- To ignore a poor performance situation is to be unfair to yourself and other employees who may have to pick up the slack created by an unproductive employee.

If we all think of discipline problems as development opportunities, we will correctly focus our energies on communicating effectively about performance.

SUMMARY

In the final analysis, a manager is not a psychiatrist, a magician, or the best friend of every employee. He or she manages performance. It is as simple as that.

He or she accomplishes this by exercising groups of skills: planning, organizing, influencing, and controlling, which make it possible to communicate frequently and clearly about performance.

Your performance management system, whether provided to you by your company or developed by yourself, should presume to develop each employee to their fullest potential. If an employee fails to respond to this approach, your alternative is a progressive disciplinary approach. These two approaches offer a wide range of messages that differ in content and style and which, when communicated clearly, will promote the desired performance.

The final chapter contains a brief examination of a wide variety of performance problems and suggestions for effective remedies by applying what you have learned.

9

Troubleshooting Performance Problems: Case Studies

Management is not a science. It is an imprecise art, applied to people and events that are uncontrollable and unpredictable. The goal of management is not simply to minimize problems or inefficiencies; it is to lead the organization forward in spite of problems and inefficiencies.

Imagine that you are a facilities manager and your department has been assigned to implement a new toxic substance control system. This is an important project that can help the company protect the environment while lowering the costs of future liabilities. It is clearly a high-priority project with extra visibility to boost your career. Even though you may take extra time to plan, staff, motivate, and monitor this project, you know your work may be set back by the following:

- new information from inside or outside the company
- employees failing to do what they promised to do
- employees doing less than they committed to do, or doing their work in a way that is different from what you expected
- schedule or budget limitations imposed on you by someone else
- other corporate priorities that conflict

It's unrealistic to expect yourself to anticipate every factor affecting every employee and manage so that there are no problems. Business management—and life—are just not that tidy. Sooner or later, as you set about to achieve your group's objectives by planning, organizing, influencing, and controlling the work of others and communicating about performance, people problems will crop up.

This final chapter offers some examples of situations you may find troublesome. Some of these problems require you to act immediately, such as those affecting safety, discipline, budgeting, and scheduling. Other problems, like inadequate training, low morale, and poor communication, sneak up on you over a long period of time, bleeding the organization's profits because of bad habits left unchallenged too long.

The suggested remedies that follow the examples apply the principles of supervision, the four functions of management, and key performance communication skills. These are useful frames of reference to get you started on solutions to similar problems of your own.

This chapter also includes general guidelines about discipline and termination to help you approach problem situations in a logical, fair, and legally defensible manner.

Before we look at prescriptions for specific types of problems, let's look at an approach that works when troubleshooting most types of problems.

TURNING COMMON SENSE INTO COMMON PRACTICE

Your common sense and good judgment are two of your best problem-solving tools. Think about what you already know about the problems you have to troubleshoot as a manager. They share characteristics with which you are well acquainted:

Poor performance. Most problems are manageable when viewed as performance problems rather than personality problems. You have at least some influence and control over the behaviors and measurable results of your workers; you cannot affect their attitudes or thoughts.

Poor communication about performance. Misunderstandings are inevitable when people are not communicating clearly or completely. Coworkers need effective communication to understand what to do and how to do it. Not everyone has to agree with everyone else, but they have to understand each other.

Conflicting or confusing expectations. When people do not know what is expected of them, they become insecure and defensive about their actions. Most people genuinely want to meet the expectations of those around them—as soon as they can discover what those expectations are! When performance expectations are met, most problems go away or find their own solutions.

Conflicting or confusing priorities or processes. If your workers are unclear about the organization's priorities or processes, they will make incorrect decisions which they may later regret. After repeating what they perceive as errors, they may cease to contribute by delegating upward or deferring to others so that someone else takes their responsibilities. This fosters employees' dependence on you, making them reluctant to decide or act without getting your approval. In turn, this situation can cause an organization to stagnate and shun new ideas.

Surprises. No one likes surprises, including your employees. Their experience has taught them that most surprises are unpleasant (unwanted transfers, layoffs, bad reports, and complaints). If they have not been forewarned or given time to prepare, you can assume you have taken one big step *away* from a solution. There are lots of ways to signal to people that you are unsatisfied with their performance; your challenge is to find the one that gets the messasge understood clearly and quickly.

I call these basic problems the *Frustrating Five* because one or more of them always seem to be present. They wear a hundred different masks in the workplace, but you will recognize them when you look below the surface of a problem situation. Do your employees feel alienated? Angry? Defensive? Reluctant to risk participating? Are they acting out their feelings at your expense? How many of your management problems are rooted in one or more of the Frustrating Five?

Common sense suggests that everything you can do to remedy the Frustrating Five is highly beneficial: Focus on the measurable performance issues first. Take time to give feedback about performance. Clarify expectations and priorities whenever they change. Avoid surprises.

Common sense is often uncommon practice, however. To uncover the Frustrating Five and develop a remedy to these common ills, I suggest you approach each problem by first answering the following sequence of questions:

1. Whose problem is this? (If I can do something to affect the solution, it's at least partially my problem.)

2. How does this problem affect performance? (If it doesn't, perhaps I should not let myself be distracted by it.)

3. Are performance expectations clearly understood by everyone? (If not, why not? Sooner or later, the differences have to be discussed.)

4. Is it clear how this performance contributes to the organization's priorities? (Explain what is important to the organization and why.)

5. What commitments have been made? (Business communication is a cycle of requests and promises.)

6. What is the gap between expected and actual peformance? (Does everyone understand my description of the problem?)

7. What are each person's suggestions for solving this problem? (Get everyone involved and committed to a resolution.)

8. What have we decided to do? (Talk is not enough; a clear decision is the best protection against the reappearance of this problem.)

Pretty basic stuff, right? Using common sense, fairness, clear communication, and mutual respect, let's look at approaches to the following problems that affect performance.

PROBLEMS THAT AFFECT PERFORMANCE

Problems Between People

Problem: Failure to live up to commitments
Situation: You like Scott as a person, but he's driving you crazy because he makes and breaks commit-

ments so casually. How can you persuade him to follow through on his share of agreements?

Suggestions: Scott likes to please people, so he is quick to say what he thinks you want to hear. He may not understand how *dis*pleased you are when he plays fast and loose with commitments. To take four steps forward (a) express your frustration and disappointment each time he lets you down, (b) express your pleasure when he follows through as you both agreed, (c) structure your conversations so that you make all requests and promises *very* clear (remind him that requests and promises are the language, the social currency, of business), and (d) finally, do not shelter Scott from the consequences of his poor decisions about his relationships. Like money or an opportunity poorly spent, Scott may not miss the integrity of his relationships until its gone.

Problem: Sexual harassment

Situation: An employee has complained about the distincty sexual nature of another employee's comments or actions. You don't want to lose either employee.

Suggestions: Discuss the complaint with the offending employee immediately; he (or she) is alleged to be inflicting abuse on a co-worker, and you and the company cannot and will not allow any harassing behavior. Sexual harassment is not the same as sexual discrimination, which directly or indirectly treats employees unfairly based on gender. Sexual harassment is assault, and employers must regard it the same way as physical abuse. After you are aware of it, you must take action. Seek the advice of your personnel manager immediately for your specific policy. The employee's complaint may become a lawsuit, so begin documenting every conversation, action, and agreement that demonstrates that you took the complaint seriously and made a genuine effort to rectify the situation. You can expect anyone accused of sexual harassment to deny any malicious intent, dismissing the charges as a misunderstanding. Perhaps this is a case of simple misunderstanding; you cannot be a judge or jury, but you can facilitate their discussions that may lead to a simple resolution. As their manager, you must alert both employees that accusations like these have destroyed careers and will not be taken lightly by the company. You must tell them both that you will not allow someone to be vilified by unsupported accusations; nor will you allow harassment to continue.

Problem: An ongoing conflict between two employees who are peers

Situation: Mary and Mark do not like each other and have demonstrated an inability to work together effectively. Left apart, they are fine workers, but the nature of their work requires them to occasionally join forces as a team. Are they allowed to continue to make life miserable for each other and the rest of the team, or does one or both of them have to leave?

Suggestions: You cannot control anyone's feelings or attitude, but you have a lot to say about their performance. Make it clear to each of them that their poor attitudes are affecting their performance ratings and the productivity of the team; consequently, if they cannot work out their differences like mature adults, you will have to make the decisions for them. By explaining the "larger picture," you are giving them the opportunity to resolve the problem independently of you, which will, of course, result in a more permanent solution. At the same time, you are laying the necessary groundwork for termination of one or both should it become necessary.

Safety Problems

Problem: Alcohol or drug abuse
Situation: No one can deny that substance abuse is a serious offense for the manager involved. About 10% of the population can be classified as "problem drinkers" or "alcoholics," and some of these people may work for you. The number of people abusing other substances is also growing, although estimates vary widely from industry to industry. The chances are very good that you will have to deal with this issue sometime in your supervisory career.
Suggestions: Begin to document specific instances in which you observed the employee on the job in an impaired condition. Consult with your personnel department or employee assistance counselor. Following are some of the major questions and considerations that will arise:

> *Is performance negatively affected?* If you cannot document poor or deteriorating performance, it will be very difficult to defend any disciplinary action you might take. As the abuse problem continues and/or increases, it will certainly have an effect on general performance,

lateness, or absenteeism at some point. If these symptoms are present, they can become the basis for disciplinary action.

Should you confront the employee directly about his or her abuse? Probably not. The employee is likely to deny the accusation and you may succeed only in cutting off communication. If the situation escalates to intervention by a third party (yes, the employee may sue you), your lack of experience in making clinical assessments will undercut your defense. Generally, it is best not to use words or phrases to the employee such as "drunk," "stoned," "on something," "how many did you have?" Your discussion with the employee should be limited to what you see—deteriorating performance, patterns of lateness or absenteeism, impaired physical condition, and so on.

If an employee reports for work obviously under the influence of either alcohol or drugs, you should:

- Describe to the employee what you observe: slurred speech, incoherence, inappropriate responses, poor reflexes, red eyes, loud voice, inability to focus, silliness, or other unusual behavior.
- Tell the employee that it is your judgment that he or she is incapable or working safely and you, therefore, will not allow him or her to go to work.
- If you have access to a medical facility, insist that the employee see a doctor or nurse. The employee can legitimately refuse, but if he or she does com-

ply, then trained medical personnel can diagnose alcohol or drug abuse.

- Tell the employee that you will make alternate transportation arrangements. You or a co-worker, security personnel, family member, police officer, or cab driver can be enlisted to take the employee home. Do not let the employee drive himself home without making such an offer. If you do, your employer may be liable if there is an accident. Making such an offer is the right and safe action to take, and it strengthens your employer's defense if you are sued for liability. Later, tell the employee that you are concerned about the situation and strongly suggest that he see a doctor or counselor.
- Involve the employee assistance counselor in this situation as soon as possible.

Problem: Horseplay and other hazardous behavior

Situation: The possibility of injury to the employee or his or her co-workers makes horseplay or the like a serious violation of the rules. If, however, horseplay has been tolerated or condoned in the past, you will have difficulty upholding any disciplinary action.

Suggestions: Standardize and publicize safety rules that clearly prohibit unsafe activities. Explain the disciplinary consequences for violation of these rules, and then make your position credible by strict enforcement. Expect that new rules will be tested until they are demonstrated to be supported by management. Safety rules should be practical, enforceable, and consistent.

On-the-Job Problems

Problem: Poor retention of superior employees

Situation: Bernard, Hans, and Ruth are bright and capable workers who recently expressed a desire to move on to bigger and better assignments. Because the company was unable to offer them what they wanted, they all quit the company. How can a manager attract and hold good employees?

Suggestions: It's been said that good employees won't stay and poor employees won't leave. Retaining quality people long enough to recoup the company's investment in them will challenge you to challenge them. By enriching their jobs with lateral assignments, special projects, cross-training, and advanced training, you can keep them from outgrowing their job too soon. You can also help retention by keeping their advancement expectations realistic; do not "sell" them on a rosy, but unlikely, future because they will only become frustrated with you and the company sooner. Finally, look for other ways the company can meet their personal needs without promoting them or granting high pay increases, such as enhanced benefit packages, extra professional exposure or recognition, and personal relationships that inspire loyalty and commitment to the company's "larger mission."

Problem: Unacceptable quantity or quality of work

Situation: Shirley is a well-intentioned lab technician, but lacks some of the important skills required to do her job. Jeff, on the other hand, has the skills to do fine carpentry work, but has an attitude problem that slows him down and makes him careless.

Suggestions: Shirley has a "can't do" problem; she lacks skills that she can acquire through training. Jeff has a "won't do" problem; he has the skills and knowledge he needs and his performance has been acceptable in the past, but he apparently lacks motivation. In each type of case, you must (a) communicate clear performance expectations and (b) establish a performance pattern conflicting with those expectations. From this framework, you can direct—even insist—on changes. Shirley must demonstrate proficiency; Jeff must exhibit new behaviors. Also, there must be consequences for poor performance: Either proactive attempts to improve skills, for example, or reactive demotions, transfers, withholding of raises and promotions, or increased accountability ("I want to meet with you twice a week until this situation is corrected."). Termination is possible.

Problem: Excessive absenteeism or tardiness

Situation: A five-man repair crew has developed some bad habits. As a group, they have a higher-than-normal absenteeism rate, and they have been observed reporting to work between 10 and 20 minutes late most mornings. Their previous supervisor did not make an issue of this because he wanted to be able to ask them to work extra time on short notice. You initially believe they should show up on time and still work the extra time; after all, the schedule and type of work is clearly outlined in the job description; they knew what they were getting into when they took their jobs and they are well paid when they work the extra hours. What should be done (if anything) about the casual work schedule?

Suggestions: First, you must decide what is considered an acceptable degree of lateness. Many managers believe that clock watching is an obstacle to getting results; others believe that if a person can be consistently late, he or she can also be consistently early; therefore, he or she can be expected to be adult enough to get themselves to work on time and do their job without making a large issue about the time clock. Approaches to this vary from organization to organization and frequently from work unit to work unit within an organization. In any case, as with other performance concerns, a pattern of unacceptable action must be documented before *any* disciplinary action can be taken.

Problem: Scheduling conflicts with shift workers

Situation: The problem of schedule conflict competes with keeping the coffee pot filled for ''problem most often discussed.'' How can you be fair to everyone unless you rotate, and how can you routinely and fairly decide a schedule that is constantly changing?

Suggestions: Don't make the problem worse than it needs to be. Hire people for specific shifts. Keep recruiting people until you find the quality people you need who prefer the less popular shifts. And don't treat them like second-class citizens, chronically short of support or direction. Rearrange your schedule so that you can see them occasionally. Whether they're nurses or printers or drivers or overseas operators, they need to know they are an important part of the organization, too.

Problem: Undeserved, but expected, pay increases

Situation: Tom may be a swell guy, but he's only a mediocre performer on a good day. Unfortunately, you have ducked the tough conversations about his disappointing performance too long, and now its time for his compensation review. Because you haven't said anything to the contrary, he believes he is doing a fine job and therefore entitled to a raise. How do you tell someone he does not get the raise he expects?

Suggestions: There is no painless way to make up in a hurry for missed opportunities to communicate about performance. Do not lose *this* opportunity to at least begin to discuss your concerns about his performance. If you do, you and the good performers on your team will continue to pay extra for mediocre performance. Give Tom less than he expects so that you get his attention, get past the "but I thought I was doing fine" part of the conversation as quickly as possible, and then help him focus on the areas of his performance that require improvement. He owes you a good day's work; you owe him clear feedback on how he's doing and fair rewards for good performance.

Problem: Falsifying records

Situation: Abigail, one of your equipment operators, is discovered to be fabricating output reports or quality control measures.

Suggestions: Falsifying records is grounds for termination or suspension, but you must be certain that she is guilty. If you allow her to remain, you are taking a risk with her future credibility (why wouldn't she do it again?), the integrity of your record-keeping system (if she can get away with it, why can't others?), and the results of your department (quality or quantity of output may suffer because you obviously don't take the reports or measures seriously). Whether she stays or goes, you must document the incident and the substance of your discussion with her.

Problem: Insubordination

Situation: Frank is your estimator, but he is not your friend. One day, without any obvious reason, he refuses to provide you with a quote. You say: "Excuse me? I mean I want you to do this now." He dismisses your request with a flip remark and saunters off. It is obvious to you that he is testing your authority. Good estimators are hard to find; should you just let this pass?

Suggestions: Insubordination is not insolence. True insubordination is the outright refusal to carry out a legitimate direct order. If the manager's request is within the subordinate's assigned duties and if it does not place the employee in a demeaning or unsafe position, the request is considered legitimate and must be carried out immediately. If the employee contends that your request is unsafe, you should refer to the safety manual. If that is not clear or if the employee still objects, immediately involve your safety officer or a higher level manager.

Problem: Lack of teamlike attitude among work group members

Situation: Personality conflicts are bogging down your work team. Everyone seems to be having a bad day, every day. Egos are commonly getting in the way of performance, and productivity is suffering.
Suggestions: It's time for some team-building exercises that cause your people to recognize and work for common group goals. Contact your personnel or training department representative for exercises that might work for your group, or consult the resources at your local library.

Problem: Stealing

Situation: Eric has been caught in the act of pilfering company property. He says this is the first time he has ever stolen and he'll never do it again. You want to punish him. What can you do?
Suggestions: As long as the incident is documented, this is justification for immediate discharge. You can recover some of the loss by using this incident to reevaluate your security procedures. Are your people naively allowing a "come and get it" attitude to prevail?

Problem: Neglect or negligence

Situation: A press operator damages a switch that requires several days and thousands of dollars to repair. Meanwhile, the schedule is thrown into turmoil and several other workers stand idle. You are angry and frustrated. What should you take into consideration before summarily firing this operator?

Suggestions: Cool off, then trust your judgment. How strong a disciplinary action you can take depends on the direct and indirect costs caused by the employee's action and whether or not the action was willful. If this operator is normally a conscientious and valued employee, minimize the damage and try to keep everyone productive while the equipment is being repaired. If this is not the first time something like this has happened, you may be dealing with an inattentive, thoughtless, or even dangerous employee. If this employee is an accident waiting to happen, be grateful no one was injured or killed, document the incident, and terminate him.

Problem: Abusive language

Situation: Ruth does not consider herself unusually sensitive or prudish, but she has finally complained to you about a co-worker who apparently uses inappropriate language routinely. Sometimes the language is just mild cursing, other times it is to or about co-workers or customers. How much can you expect to change this type of behavior?

Suggestions: Discuss this problem immediately with the offending employee to get the other side of the story. Establish this as a performance problem by linking it to the negative reactions of co-workers and customers. Clarify your expectations; as with chronic lateness and excessive absenteeism, a pattern of unacceptable behavior must be established before any disciplinary action can be taken.

SUMMARY

Remember that the best management techniques are those that work for you. Every new situation and each difficult conversation are learning opportunities for you. Do not be shy about making mistakes. Experiment. If a new approach seems to make sense, try it. Although you may not be able to avoid all difficult situations, you can reasonably expect this of yourself: Most of your people should be well managed most of the time.

Appendix A
The Manager's Toolkit:
The Rules of the Management Game

1. You will receive opportunities. You must pre-
    pare for them. They will continue to come
    as long as you are ready. Some may not look
    like opportunities at the time, and some will
    be better than others. You cannot take care
    of all of them properly, so you must carefully
    choose the best and forget about the rest.

2. There are no mistakes, only lessons.

3. A lesson is repeated until learned. A lesson
    will be presented to you in various forms until

you have learned it. When you have learned it, you can go on to the next lesson. Learning lessons does not end.

4. There is never enough time.

5. There is never enough information.

6. There will always be a better way, but there is never a better time than now.

7. Ask always: Is there a better way to do this?

8. Project confidence. Soon, you may even feel confident.

9. Never embarrass your boss.

10. Tell your people to tell you about problems before they embarrass you.

11. Deliver bad news as soon as possible.

12. Your credibility is made up of requests and promises. Learn to make and keep both, and don't waste either.

13. Getting it done is what it is all about.

14. While money isn't everything in all cases, in business it's the only thing. Taking care of your customers and your people just happen to be good business.

15. Avoid surprises, except those that are pleasant surprises for your customer, such as delivering early.

16. The customer's needs come first, your people's needs are next, and your needs rarely matter.

17. Keep the big picture in focus.

18. That which is measured is improved.

19. Your expectations of others become true.

20. Your answers lie within you. You get to make all the important choices.

21. Every problem has another one behind it; so seek permanent solutions to avoid repeating yourself.

22. There is no virtue in being a moving target. Stand and be counted.

NOW YOU ARE A MANAGER. YOUR JOB IS TO

- get the expected results from your work group
- see the "big picture"
- work through others
- get and give more information
- solve problems
- work with other managers
- work as one of many partners in the success of the business

---

Questions to ask early:

> What is your job here? Do you like your job?
>
> What do you especially like or dislike about your job? How do you know when you are doing your job well?
>
> What does this department do?
>
> How does this department get evaluated?
>
> Who are the customers of this department, both inside and outside the company, and what are they saying about us?

Questions to ask later:

> How are we doing?
>
> What obstacles are keeping us from serving our customers—both internal and external—in the ways they want us to?
>
> Do we share a common, accurate understanding of what is really going on around here?
>
> Do we share a common vision of who we are?
>
> Do we agree what our priorities are?
>
> What are our plans for the next three days? The next three weeks? The next three months?

Appendix B
The Manager's Toolkit:
Getting Started

What will you do the first day of your new job? The first week? The first month? Below is a list of almost-serious suggestions about what you should be doing to make those first impressions the right impressions and those first steps the right steps. Even though you will probably stumble once or twice in the early months, you will at least fall in the right direction!

Day 1

All of the following may need to be done today. Which will you choose to do, and in which order?

_____ introduce myself to everyone in my work group

_____ refurnish my office with Italian sculpture

_____ familiarize myself with the records, schedules, budgets, and plans of the person who sat in this chair up until last week; if I can't read them all today, I'll at least know where to find them.

_____ take a slow tour of the office and/or plant to familiarize myself with "the feel of the place" and present myself to the work group as a "real" person

_____ start a list of problems I observe, usually including inefficiencies that I think I see or know about (I will NOT take action on these problems yet—I won't even mention them to anyone—because you haven't the time or wherewithal to verify these as problems yet)

_____ start a list of opportunities I observe (this list includes my ideas for saving money and making money); I'll keep this list to myself, too.

_____ figure out how the phone works; introduce myself to the person who can help me master it in the coming weeks.

_____ learn how to turn the computer on and off; also learn who knows how to make the system do what it is supposed to do. Resolve in future to improve productivity by saving looking-up time, putting-away time, cross-referencing time, writing time, and number-crunching time

_____ sit in on one of my subordinate's meetings; LISTEN

_____ move into my "space" and make it mine with at least one personal object that will get conversations started (such as a photo of my hunting dogs or my favorite vacation island)

_____ resolve NOT to make promises I cannot absolutely, positively keep, no matter how tempting it is

_____ resolve NOT to make changes in anything for at least a few weeks, which will give me enough time to consult with the "stakeholders"—those people with interests in what I change

_____ begin reading everything I can get my hands on, looking for meaningful information about our products and services, customers, and people

Week 1

All the following may need to be done this week. Which will you choose to do, and in which order?

_____ begin planning immediately how to learn what my department does, how it does it, how much it costs to do, and how good it is; I know that in the not-too-distant-future, I will be asked to make scheduling commitments, product production estimates, manpower calculations, and much more. . . . I want and need to become the resident expert on my department, so learning about this job and this department is my number one priority.

_____ begin making requests of others inside and outside the department for information; if I don't get the information promised to me, I ask again.

_____ meet casually with each employee for light conversation to learn their name and title, what they do, and a little about them as individuals, I go to them on company time; I do NOT ask them to give up their break time to come and talk to me

_____ meet with each employee again to ask open-ended questions like the following; remain noncommittal because I am not sure what really needs to be changed yet, if anything:

    a. what parts of your job do you really enjoy (Don't ask for the negative aspects yet, but don't be surprised if they tell you anyway.)

    b. what suggestions do you have to improve things around here?

    c. how do you interact with the other people in this work unit? (Strive to approach employees in a nonthreatening, constructive manner so they will feel comfortable sharing their thoughts with you. If you cause them to become defensive, you'll get worse than nothing: excuses and bad attitudes.)

_____ meet with my counterparts in other divisions to share experiences, anecdotes, and useful tips; these people will become part of my new network

_____ meet with the Corporate Furnishings Department about repainting the sign on my reserved parking place

_____ select three moderately important and difficult problems to solve this week; then, line them up in order of their importance to the company's goals and solve them completely, one at a time (This provides first-hand experience with how things really work in the department.)

_____ meet with my boss several times to discuss his short- and long-term priorities; find out how he thinks and what he values so I can be sure to meet his needs and "manage my manager"

_____ continue plowing through the production reports and personnel reports found in the files; I have decided that I must get somewhat familiar with these things quickly, even if I don't fully understand the significance of what I'm looking at yet. I'm not asking subordinates to filter the information because I want to "get my fingers dirty" first and ask questions later, after I understand it better.

Month 1

All the following may need to be done this month. Which will you choose to do, and in which order?

_____ embark on a mission of cleanliness to tidy all the bulletin boards in the department

_____ continue follow-up meetings with employees who have something to say about some aspect of our problems; I remain the Sympathetic Information Gatherer and resist the temptation to "fix things" just because someone asked me to, so I think I am building a reputation for (a) being a good listener and (b) thinking before acting

_____ continue to add to my lists of problems and lists of opportunities (see Day 1)

_____ continue to select problems and opportunities requiring action and tackling them completely so they are "finished" in one way or another; I fear getting lots of things started and getting nothing done. I think I am getting a nice reputation for being a "finisher," so people seem to be gaining confidence in me.

_____ finish my reading of "random" and general information; now I know what information is most relevant and I have assigned myself a short reading list that will keep me abreast of industry, company, and department news and performance

_____ resist the temptation to get drawn into the traps that will take too much of my time; there is so much yet to learn, and I can't slow down now!

Appendix C
The Manager's
Toolkit:
Personal Planning
Skills

To apply the planning skills discussed in Chapter 4, take at least the following actions:

_____ Obtain your job description from your manager or the human resources department; clarify any inconsistencies or points of confusion with your boss now, while there is still time to make adjustments.

_____ Ask your boss what his expectations are. Which project or program is he watching closely? Of course, as you make your own plans, you will want to pay special attention to these.

_____ Talk to your employees and ask them: "What plans are underway for which projects?" "What problems with scheduling, budgeting, or delivery do you foresee, and what are your recommendations to solve the problems?" This will help alert you to plans made or not made by your predecessor and prevent surprises.

_____ Obtain the formal and informal, written and unwritten, short-, mid-, and long-term plans that involve your department. Do you understand the organization's objectives and priorities? You need information now, so keep asking the people who can give it to you.

_____ Begin making short-term plans for yourself immediately, and stick to them. Plan your day, your week, your month as if your job depended on your ability to plan and follow through.

_____ Finally, make sure that you keep the work moving and keep those around you well-informed about what you are doing. If you discover that you cannot accomplish something for which someone else did the planning, communicate your scheduling problems immediately. Do not let yourself be victimized by someone else's plan; seize control as soon as you can, make the plans your plans, and begin building your reputation as a planner who can be relied upon.

TIPS TO MANAGE YOUR TIME

It's the end of the day. You've taken one too many phone calls and sat through one too many meetings. You're tired and frustrated—where did the day go? Why can't you get done what you planned to do?

Your problem lies partially in the nature of your position. You're on the spot for everyone, so you're their target, friend, source of information and permission; it's no wonder you occasionally feel beleaguered.

Your problem may also stem from less-than-perfect control of your time. DANGER: THIS CAN KILL YOUR CAREER, one minute at a time.

Many books and courses about time management are available. The best of them talk about getting the best return for spending your time resources, not just how to be more efficient. The key to time management is effectiveness: It is far better that you do the right things inefficiently than do the wrong things efficiently.

The following suggestions will help you get started:

1. Practice managing for short periods of time, then expand your control as you get better at it. You're probably already doing this when you have an important and well-defined project. Feel confidence from the fact that you have done this before on a small scale. You can do this.

2. Spend your best time on the important stuff.

3. Beware of the time wasters. They live where you work. Sometimes they look like friends and employees; sometimes they are old habits and comfortable routines.

4. Make the hard decisions. Delay can paralyze you because it becomes its own reward.

5. Solve the tough problems. Fretting about too many problems slows everything down.

6. Delegate. Managers get results by working through others.

7. Stick to your plan. It's a good one—certainly better than no plan. The largest benefit of your plan is to remind you what is most important to do, so your time is always well directed toward the work that matters most.

HOW WELL ARE YOU MANAGING YOUR PERSONAL CAREER?

The five keys to successful personal planning are specificity, feasibility, a control system that updates the plan, writing the plan down, and periodic reviews of the plan.

The following questions will help you summarize your personal career plans; note if they are or are not supportive of your plans for your department or division!

1. Do you believe you can influence the future through your planning efforts, or is success a matter of luck?

2. Do you understand the similarities between planning for the business and planning your career? How are they different?

3. Explain how you go about "inventing" the successes in your career. Are you a successful planner?

4. Have you had to adapt your career plans recently to accommodate new information or a new situation? Do you still have confidence in your planning process? What have you learned from this experience and has it caused you to change your personal planning process?

5. What is your personal mission statement?

6. What are your three- to five-year goals?

7. Describe what you want to happen during the next 12 months:

8. What are your three top priorities?

9. What are the dangers of spending too much time planning? (*Clue:* Rather than compressing all your planning activities into a single marathon session, it is better to spread them

out over several days or weeks so you have time to let ideas develop—and limit the plan to just two pages!)

10. How do you know when you are not following your plan?

11. When is the next time you are going to review your career and life plan?

Appendix D
The Manager's Toolkit:
The Art of Delegating

"If you ride a horse, sit close and tight. If you ride a man, sit easy and light." Poor Richard's Almanac

You've heard this before: "If you want something done, ask the busy man. He'll find time to do it." There may be a grain of truth in this, but it is not what being a manager is all about.

Managing means achieving the organization's goals by working through others. The only way this is going to happen is through effective delegation: the entrusting of your authority to a representative. When you delegate, you confer your authority to make certain decisions on a person willing to accept the short-term responsibility for completing a task. Because they have a portion of your authority, they can act and fulfill their responsibility.

The integrity of the delegation process is protected by accountabilities transferred to your representative with the authority and responsibility. If this representative fails to perform, he or she will be held accountable and will suffer predictable negative consequences.

Delegation is more than just handing out a job and walking away; Robert B. Nelson, author of *DELEGATION: The Power of Letting Go,* says it requires four steps:

Prepare to delegate.   You must select the right person to assign the responsibility, and then you must mentally prepare to let go of any emotional investment you have in this responsibility. If you can successfully force yourself to disengage from the task you are delegating, you will stay out of the way and let your representative do the job while you move on to other tasks that only you can do.

Delegate.   You need to seek agreement with your representative about the goals, performance expectations, level of authority, support of other team members, and positive and negative consequences for good or poor performance.

Monitor the delegation.   You must stay in touch with your representative in order to provide feedback. You play a critical coaching role here.

Evaluate the delegation.   How did each of you perform during this activity? Was it a win–win situation, or was someone disappointed? Would both of you do this again?

You MUST learn to delegate. Delegation will allow you to rise above the limitations of your personal time and ability. By letting go of your tasks, which can be and should be done more efficiently by others, you put everyone's talents to better use.

1. If your supervisor tells you that the organization is "centralized," what can you assume about the decision-making process?

2. Personally, what is your strongest base of personal power within the informal organization?

3. What types of questions will you direct to your supervisor? Your colleagues? A technical expert?

4. You need extra help or extra information from someone outside your department. How can you get it?

5. If you accept the responsibility for an assignment, but your supervisor withholds the authority, what are your chances for success?

6. Personally, are you more comfortable in a line or a staff position?

7. Do you like to have tasks delegated to you? Why?

8. Organizations are getting more complex, often causing employees to report to several supervisors concurrently. It can be argued that this actually diminishes the control over the employee. What does this require the employee to do relative to his or her job description?

9. Describe an organization with which you are familiar that can be described as "running smoothly." What makes this possible?

10. Describe an organization you are familiar with that is not operating well. How do you know it's having problems, and what would you recommend to remedy the situation?

Appendix E
The Manager's
Toolkit:
Resolving Conflict

Guess what? No matter how hard you try, not everyone in your work unit is going to agree. Conflicts are bound to arise because people have incompatible agendas, or at least they perceive that they do.

The principles of supervision we explored can be valuable guides to resolving conflicts that keep the organization from being effective.

Briefly, the process of conflict resolution can be described as a compromise between individual goals and organizational goals. The organization's goal is to function smoothly in the pursuit of its objectives; the goal of the individual employee is to have his or her personal needs for job satisfaction and financial security met.

The principles of supervision are helpful because they organize the organization. This goes a long way toward minimizing the conflict that accompanies organizational confusion. By applying the principles of supervision, you can answer questions like, "Who's responsible for this?" and "Did you have the authority to make that decision?"

WHERE ELSE DOES CONFLICT COME FROM?

The organization versus the individual is only one of the potential conflicts in the workplace. Other conflicts include co-worker and co-worker ("I don't like you and I don't like working with you"), worker and manager ("I disagree"), society and the organization ("stop polluting") and the organization and the government ("comply or pay the penalties"), just to name a few. The same process of goal and attitude compromise works to resolve conflict between these groups. Two co-workers, for example, may disagree on how a certain job should be done. Whereas one worker wants to do the job in the shortest time period possible, the other wants to do the highest quality job possible, regardless of the time it takes. Each is focused on the same task, but each sees the most important part of the task differently. To resolve the conflict and work together, each worker must be able to identify the other's goals and attitudes and reconcile them with his own.

Positive Effects of Conflict at Work

Conflict is a natural element of any workplace. It is a by-product of the interaction between people with different ideas. As long as conflict can be resolved in a healthy, constructive, and orderly manner, short- and long-term benefits will result for those involved.

The following are some examples of how conflict and conflict resolution can be beneficial to both the individual and the organization:

> *New ideas.* Jim was anxious to prove himself in the engineering department, and argued persuasively to have new materials he learned about in school specified in a new product proposal the department is submitting. Dan, who had worked for the company longer, was threatened by Jim's ambition and had fought him hard on the material specification.
>
> As the deadline for the proposal draws near, both Jim and Dan realized that they had to resolve their differences. Although they both had good reasons for using their chosen materials, both also had to admit that there were strong reasons to look for an alternative material. After a frank discussion, they jointly commit themselves to finding the best material to specify by reviewing all the important characteristics required for the product. The hardest task was ranking the importance of these characteristics in the order of their importance to the project instead of by self-serving personal preference. They agreed to discuss each point until they agreed. They both realized that if their personal ideas could not stand up under tough scrutiny, the ideas had to be improved.

In the end, an entirely different material was found for the product specification. The new material was better than either of their personal favorites, and they admitted that they would not have considered the new material if they were not challenged to defend their first selections. An added bonus to the experience was a new respect for each other's professional abilities.

Quality control. The Miracle Drug Company was having a difficult time getting its new wonder drug approved by the FDA for distribution and sale because of prior quality control problems related to earlier product launches by the company. Suspicious of yet another problem, the FDA officials were particularly wary.

The company management contended that all quality control problems stemmed from vague test and control regulations that often seemed contradictory. Both parties had taken great offense upon reading summary statements attributed to each other in a series of newspaper articles about the controversy. Trust and communication were breaking down, and the drug itself was receiving less and less attention. Finally, after many months without progress, the company replaced the product managers who were shepherding the product through the approval process.

The new managers moved quickly to resolve the conflict between the company and the government. First, they examined the quality control procedures in the company's manufacturing process. The FDA's suspicions were at least partly justified. Changes were made to improve the weak links in the process. Then they scheduled an informal meeting with the regulators. They clearly outlined the company's goal: to gain approval for the manufacture and sale of the drug. They specified the requirements that they did not understand and requested clarification.

The FDA responded, but was still suspicious. After the company's product managers were certain that they were in compliance, they requested another inspection by the FDA inspectors.

The inspection was the longest and most careful the company had ever undergone, but the FDA agreed that the company's procedures had passed with flying colors. The FDA explained that they had never really questioned the scientific basis for the drug; their reluctance to approve was rooted in their suspicion of the quality control procedures. The agency inspectors admitted that they did not make compliance easy with regulations that could be misinterpreted or appeared to be in conflict with each other, and they agreed to publish clarification for the benefit of other companies.

Improving productivity. Alan was struggling with an internal conflict that sprang from his recent promotion to inspector of his company's medical product. Because Alan did much of the design work on the project, he felt particularly close to each phase of production and knew what to watch for.

It became apparent, however, that Alan was not fast enough in his inspection. Alan's manager indicated that if Alan did not or could not complete his inspections faster, the problem would be taken out of his hands.

"I trust you to be using your time conscientiously, but the bottleneck in your department is putting us way behind our deliveries," warned Alan's manager.

Alan was worried about missing a critical test and sending out a faulty product. He argued persuasively that he was the first inspector for this product, and because the product was to be used in hospital emergency rooms, the company's reputation and the lives of accident victims were at stake. Alan had begun to stay after work without pay to get caught up, which led to numerous arguments with his wife and daily tension headaches. His anxiety caused him to go even slower, and his productivity was deteriorating instead of improving.

Finally, Alan had had enough. He knew something had to give. Late one night, he faced the truth: He cared too much about "his" product and had too much of a personal emotional investment in it. He realized that he must wash his hands of it entirely, quit or get fired, or devise a better inspection procedure.

Within a few days, his productivity improved dramatically. Without compromising the critical tests he must perform, he had identified many that could be handled elsewhere on the production line by the line supervisors. He had even eliminated some altogether. He began to relax, and his personal productivity improved even more. Soon, he would be ready to turn over his responsibilities and go on to his next assignment.

Improving workplace relationships. Fred and Abdul took an immediate dislike to each other. They each seemed to represent to the other much of what each disliked about the world. Unfortunately, they both needed a job and ended up working across from each other in a small office.

Tension grew daily. Every motion, every comment became a bullet in an undeclared private war. Both began to show signs of fatigue, anxiety, and poor production.

Almost simultaneously, Fred and Abdul heard each other reprimanded by their respective supervisors for disappointing performance. Sensing finally that they were seriously affecting each other in a negative way, they began to change. They began to speak more freely, gradually learning to respect each other. Friendly competition replaced unfounded first impressions.

The conflict between Fred and Abdul forced them to change their behavior toward each other or suffer severe personal consequences. Their attitudes may not have changed, but their relationship with each other improved substantially because they each had a vested interest in resolving the conflict between them.

In each of these cases, there was a conflict between opposing factions in the work force. In the course of the daily routine, these conflicts were resolved, leading to direct benefits for those involved. These cases are not unusual in any way; they illustrate that conflict and conflict resolution are normal in the workplace environment and exist at every level.

NEGATIVE EFFECTS OF CONFLICT AT WORK

Conflicts that cannot be resolved have varying negative effects in the workplace. When a conflict cannot be resolved or is resolved in a manner unacceptable to one or more of the opposing factions, a stressful situation develops, which keeps the organization or the individual from functioning effectively.

One of the first negative effects of conflict manifests itself in a decline in productivity, which is often due to loss of incentive or to stress.

Another negative effect of conflict is one or more inappropriate behavioral responses to the conflict situations, which in turn leads to negative behavior that will probably cause more conflict. This could be expected, for example, if an employee submitted a new idea to resolve a production problem and the supervisor flatly ignored the employee's input without discussing the merits of the idea. The employee naturally would feel frustrated that his input was not appreciated or valued and might adopt an "I don't care" attitude, which in turn affects his performance. A more appropriate response for the employee would be to bring the idea up at a later time or regard it in a less personal way.

The following are some of the other negative behavioral responses to conflict situations:

1. Excessive absenteeism

2. Unsociable behavior in the workplace

3. Increased conflicts between co-workers, especially over seemingly petty matters

4. Increased expressions of worker frustration, such as complaining about unsatisfactory conditions

5. Questioning of supervisor's authority, including direct insubordination

Of course, conflict at work is only one possible reason for negative behavior. The manager is challenged to resolve conflict in an appropriate manner so that all parties can reap the positive benefits of the experience.

Because conflict is the natural, predictable result of the clash between the goals and attitudes of the worker and the organization he works for, it is the manager's responsibility to control and resolve negative conflict as it occurs in the workplace and to prevent unnecessary conflict through appropriate planning. For example, when a company policy restricts the productivity of workers or when worker behavior affects normal operations, the manager must take decisive action to correct the situation before it triggers conflict with other parts of the group.

Remember, not all conflict is bad. Some conflicts are definitely positive. The manager's goal is not to prevent or resolve all conflicts, but rather to prevent or resolve those negative conflicts that are unproductive, unnecessary and not constructive.

The following guidelines are for determining who or what is responsible for negative workplace conflict:

Workers are responsible for

1. Declining performance levels,

2. Unacceptable workplace behavior,

3. Inadequate skill levels to perform specified tasks,

4. Inappropriate interaction among co-workers.

The company is responsible for

1. Policies or procedures that lead to declining productivity,

2. Policies or procedures that lead to worker dissatisfaction,

3. Inadequate training programs for workers,

4. Policies or procedures that factionalize the work force.

Managers are responsible for

1. Unclear translation of corporate goals,

2. Inadequate or inconsistent supervision,

3. Inadequate or inconsistent coaching, counseling, and discipline,

4. Inadequate concern for worker needs and goals.

In many cases, there is a dual responsibility for carrying out the solutions to conflict. A worker's performance may decline because of a poorly organized job definition or work station. Both the job definition and the employee's adaptation to the job must be clarified.

After the conflict is identified, the manager's responsibility is to take the necessary steps to reconcile the goal and attitude differences that will resolve the conflict. This is accomplished through confrontation, behavior modification, changes in organizational goals, or changes in the methods used to reach those goals. Finally, because conflict by its nature creates a certain amount of stress at all levels of the organization, it is the manager's responsibility to take some steps to help the individual or the organization cope with the stress.

Three distinct management styles have been identified: authoritative, humanitarian, and participative. The style used by the individual manager tends to dictate the nature and type of conflicts that occur, how conflicts are resolved, and the potential for new conflicts.

Guidelines for Conflict Resolution

The first step in resolving any conflict is to identify and clearly describe the conflict. Unacceptable workplace behavior is symptomatic of a conflict. Declining performance, for example, or absenteeism or excessive arguing with other workers are signs of conflict. In some cases, these are signs of a simple conflict which can be accepted at face value. In the case of absenteeism, the individual may have a chronic health problem that is beyond anyone's control.

However, a simple conflict may also be a symptom of a larger, more subtle, and more complex conflict. The worker may be unhappy with his job or unable to get along with co-workers or managers, or he or she may even have an alcohol or drug problem. All the manager is certain of is that he must take action to correct the inappropriate behavior. Good reason or bad, the worker is performing poorly.

Through an effective system of information gathering and performance measurement, a manager is able to identify and describe the true nature of the conflict. The information gathering process starts by noting and describing in specific detail the nature of the unacceptable behavior. If an employee is frequently late, mark it down: "Kathy was tardy on the 17th—22 minutes late." You must document the negative behavior in detail with dates and descriptions of specific incidents.

The manager must also be prepared to explain how the negative behavior is affecting the employee's work performance. Is this behavior substantially different from that of other employees in the department? Have corrective measures been attempted before? Are any other symptoms apparent that might indicate other problems?

This first stage of observation prepares the manager to confront the employee and suggests possible corrective measures to take. By now, the manager should know what the surface problem is: a conflict between the individual and the company's policy on tardiness. He knows how extensive the problem is, including the specific dates of the offenses; he also knows how serious the problem is compared with the other workers' behavior. Finally, he knows the nature of the short-term effects, including specific performance deficiencies. The questions that have yet to be answered are: Why is this behavior occurring? Is it a symptom of a larger conflict? These questions can be answered through a confrontation with the employee.

CONFRONTING THE PROBLEM EMPLOYEE

The manager MUST remember at this point that the goal is to solve a problem, not create another one with a destructive confrontation. Pick a time to meet that is as close as possible to the last offense, yet one with a minimum of anxiety for both of you. Be prepared, avoid generalities, and be constructive. Your task as manager is to correct or eliminate the problem or the problem employee.

An effective employee confrontation starts by presenting the problem from the manager's viewpoint. In the case of excessive tardiness, this means stating clearly that the employee is coming late to work on an unacceptably frequent basis and that this tardiness is affecting his performance or that it's contrary to company policy. The employee's response will be either an acceptance that the problem exists as stated by the manager or a denial of the manager's charges.

Through effective communication and the art of negotiation, managers can control confrontations with employees effectively. This is important because the person who controls the confrontation tends to have the advantage in achieving the desired outcome. The person who is not in control can be led or directed by the other person and usually has to accept some version of the other person's goals or needs.

The following is a set of rules or guidelines that managers can follow to control a confrontation effectively:

1. Be able to state and identify clearly the nature of the conflict as you perceive it. The employee must know clearly the company's position in relation to his performance.

2. Be prepared to substantiate the stated position, and anticipate the questions the employee might ask.

3. Listen carefully to the employee's response to the stated position. This response indicates the type of behavior the employee will use as a response to the confrontation.

4. Select a style of communicating with the employee that best counteracts any negative behavior by the employee. For example, if the employee denies the conflict or withdraws completely, a tact of dominance might be applicable.

5. Direct and redirect the conversation back to the nature and identity of the conflict or the

proposed resolution. This is accomplished by acknowledging statements that are not essential (for example, "Yes, I understand that other employees have been late this week," or, "I agree with you that this is a company-wide problem") and then redirecting the conversation by restating the conflict at hand ("But I want to find a way for you to be here on time," or, "But let's talk about how the problem relates to your performance"). Whenever the conversation goes in the wrong direction, redirect it back to the stated problem or the proposed resolution.

6. Eliminate personal attacks and focus on problem solving. Employees tend to rationalize a situation or try to avoid it through the use of personal attacks on the manager or other employees. Make it clear that personal attacks are not acceptable.

7. Learn to distinguish the reasons from the excuses. There are some legitimate reasons for unacceptable behavior or performance deficiencies, but excuses are just a way of avoiding problems.

It should be clear at this point that the key to effective communication in a confrontation situation is to focus on conflict identification and conflict resolution. Any communication that detracts from this goal dilutes the problem-solving process. Also, through careful listening and observation, the manager can identify clearly the tactics that are being used by the employee and can determine the correct approach to counter the employee's unacceptable responses and maintain control of the situation.

NEGOTIATING RESOLUTION TO CONFLICT

In order to reach a conclusion that is acceptable to both persons, a compromised or negotiated agreement must be reached. Effective negotiators can easily trade off points that are of secondary importance for a favorable agreement on the major points. The following guidelines will help you negotiate resolutions to conflicts:

1. Know your—or your company's—"bottom line." The bottom line is the nonnegotiable point or points beyond which you cannot compromise. Everything "above the bottom line" is negotiable.

2. Focus on negotiating the process or method that will be used to solve the problem rather than the problem itself. How an employee gets to work every day is open for negotiation. Whether the employee shows up or not is not negotiable.

3. Understand your position of strength or weakness. This involves determining whether the differences in the positions of authority change the bargaining position. Also, understand who will bear the negative consequences if a resolution is not found.

4. Give the employee an honorable method of re-
   treat. People tend to respond irrationally when
   they feel backed into a corner with no honorable way of surrendering. By presenting options
   which accomplish the same thing, a person
   feels that he has gotten out of the corner grace-
   fully because he made some choices.

5. Recognize that the purpose of negotiating is
   not to be a winner or loser, but to reach a solution that resolves the conflict. In other
   words, accomplish the goal and don't worry
   about winning the battle of words. Making a
   concession so that the other person does not
   feel like a loser is acceptable, even preferable,
   if the main goal is reached. In addition, the
   chances that the final agreement will be carried out are better if the other person retains
   his self-respect and feels that he played an important part in reaching the solution.

Negotiation plays an important part in resolving
complex problems and conflicts where it is important to have a consensus on several aspects of a conflict or when a trade-off of goals and needs is
necessary. Effective negotiators have a clear understanding of what they want to accomplish, what they
can afford to give up, and how the process of negotiation helps them achieve these goals. Effective communication and artful negotiation make the
difference between conflict situations that are laden
with stress and those which are dealt with smoothly
and firmly.

In a confrontive situation, the employee's level of stress relates directly to his feelings about how he was treated, whether he had input into the process, whether he was listened to, and whether he feels good about the solution that was reached. You will be more successful in moving the discussion forward if you can keep everyone's level of stress down (including your own!).

In order to proceed, the employee must accept the manager's stastement of the problem. The manager can draw upon his or her observation data to lead the employee to see the manager's point of view. If the employee continues to deny the problem as presented by the manager, either a conflict exists between the person and the authority of the manager (which may be the real basis for the problem), or the observation by the manager was incorrect.

After the employee and the manager have accepted a definition of the basic problem, a simple explanation by the employee can often identify and remedy the basic conflict. If the explanation does not address itself fully to the problem or if the manager feels that there is something else at the bottom of the problem, additional questioning can provide additional information. It is important for the manager to be able to interpret the employee's response and to discern signs of underlying conflict. A few probing questions may be appropriate, but usually the manager is successful if he or she simply provides an atmosphere of trust and openness. Given the opportunity, most people talk about their problems.

After you have determined the type of conflict with which you are dealing, you can set an attainable, measurable objective that will begin to remove, minimize, or correct the problem.

The manager's role at this point is one of leadership. The manager is most effective when helping to answer the question, "Where do we go from here?" People caught in conflict have difficulty seeing and appreciating the problem-solving process from their limited perspective, and a third party can provide the critical guidance when they need it most.

As a manager, you will find it necessary to keep the conflict–resolution process in the context of performance improvement. Your job is to resolve conflicts that affect the productivity of the organization. Because poor performance means lower profitability, you have a responsibility and a right to be involved. However, your responsibility does not extend very far beyond the workplace, if at all; leave the psychological counseling, domestic intervention, and advice to the lovelorn to the professionals. Your power base is tied to your authority in the workplace, and to stray too far afield is to invite misunderstandings, resentment, and compromise of your effectiveness. Simply stated, your job in conflict resolution is to represent the organization and see to it that the conflict is resolved so that maximum performance can be restored.

Appendix F
The Manager's
Toolkit:
Networking

If information is power (and it is), much of your influence depends on what you know and when you know it. You may not share the positional power of those at the top of the corporate hierarchy, but you can certainly make an important difference by mastering information about the day-to-day operations of the company.

Networking is commonly used to describe the process of giving and receiving business information through informal communication channels. Developing your information channels or network is a way for you to

- learn what changes lie ahead.
- identify problems early.
- test and presell your ideas.

- defuse potentially damaging or embarrassing situations.
- make time work for you.
- give and receive off-the-record feedback.
- learn first-hand who is and is not doing his or her job.
- suggest and solicit ideas to improve operations.
- scout future job opportunities.

The following suggestions will help you recognize and make the most of networking opportunities.

HOW DO YOU GET PEOPLE TO TALK TO YOU?

Information is not going to flow to you automatically, without some effort on your part. People are not going to pick up the phone, go out of their way, or go out on a limb to talk to you unless they sense that it is somehow in their best interests to do so. This means you have to earn their confidence and trust. If the people around you believe you to be fair and honorable, they will be more likely to confide in you.

Your position puts you on display. More people than you know are watching you. Does your "walk match your talk?" Do you keep your promises? Are you someone to be counted on? Can you hold your position, or do you just say whatever your listener wants to hear?

You have to lay some groundwork to build the kind of communication network you want. Ask yourself: Are you making it easy for people to share their thoughts with you by being

A good listener? Are you ready to be quiet and let someone else talk? Some new managers become so full of their own ideas and concerns that they unintentionally shut others out. The people around you know when you are not really listening. Practice good listening and you may be surprisesd by the thoughtfulness of their comments.

Accessible? People can't talk to you if they can't find you. If you intentionally keep a low profile or bury yourself in meetings, you are sending a clear message that you are "just too busy" to listen. Go where your people are—in the plant, in the lab, or on the road. Don't be surprised if some important information comes your way from a casual walk down the hallway with someone who just happened to be going in your direction.

Approachable? Does your style encourage people to open up, to talk, and to listen? Or are your people starting to call you "ol' stoney face" or "dragon lady" behind your back? Few of your employees probably feel comfortable complaining to or making a speech to the boss. Make it obvious to them that you are receptive to conversation around the coffeepot, to notes written on napkins, or to whatever else makes them feel comfortable.

Trustworthy? This is basic. Can you keep your employees' confidences? Do you exercise discretion? Are you known for your common sense or your loose lips? Your employees take a risk when they talk to you, and your peers and bosses take a similar risk when they include you in discussions. How do you handle the information people share with you? Sure, you may have been trustworthy in the past, but will you be in your new position? It is common for new managers to misuse information because they are struggling to cope with new pressures. If you begin to use information to impress others, for example, you can be sure people will think twice before they share with you.

Fair? You may believe you are as fair as you always have been, but your view may not jibe with the perceptions of others. You have to manage how you are perceived. Do you appear to be playing favorites? Do you give even-handed feedback about performance? Do you misappropriate the ideas of others, or say or do things that can be interpreted as hypocritical or unethical? Be careful to be fair; once judged as unfair, you will not have the luxury of frank and open appraisal to counteract this perception.

Dependable? What is your reputation for sticking by your commitments, for following through, and for keeping your promises? If you're known for your consistency and predictability, your information network will have consistency, predictability, and integrity.

HOW DO YOU GET PEOPLE TO TELL YOU BAD NEWS BEFORE IT'S TOO LATE TO DO SOMETHING ABOUT IT?

What you hear from your information sources depends on your history of responses. Your sources will predict your response to bad news based on their prior experience with you. Blame, shouting, recriminations, passing the buck, defensiveness, and similar responses are going to discourage the sharing of bad news. If this is what you really want—to never hear the bad news—then you are missing any opportunity to correct a bad situation before it gets out of hand.

The smart manager creates a supportive environment that encourages and rewards people who speak up when they see a problem. Isn't this why you're a manager in the first place, to solve problems and improve the quality of everyone's worklife?

Here are some of the steps you can take to foster an environment where people are not afraid to tell you bad news:

Be constructive. Make it clear to the messenger with bad news that you are genuinely interested in understanding all the details and getting to work on the solution.

Keep everyone informed and involved. Demonstrate respect and confidence in your employees by sharing, not hoarding, information. The people you work with want and deserve information that affects them. Well-informed employees are generally more optimistic in their outlook and more resourceful, and therefore more helpful in problem-solving. If you routinely share good news and bad news with them, they will do likewise with you.

Express interest in them as individuals. Get involved with your employees' careers. What do they really like and dislike about their jobs? What are their dreams? What do they think are their strengths? When you add a genuinely personal element to your relationship with your employees, they are more likely to do the same. If they are confident you are looking out for their interests, they will be more likely to say, "Listen, boss, there's something you ought to know about that last shipment. . . ."

Use the information you receive responsibly. Do not underestimate the power of the grapevine. Others may know more than you think, and if you misuse their information, your information network will judge you incompetent (you don't understand), irresponsible (you say things to people without regard for the consequences), or unethical (you cannot be trusted).

Provide multiple communication channels. Everyone is not comfortable making a presentation at a staff meeting, or writing a memo, or scheduling a one-on-one discussion with you, or confronting a problem head-on. You can help the people in your network by making it clear that you are receptive to their information anytime and that they can present it any way that is comfortable for them. You may even want to use a suggestion box, questionnaire, or similar device so you don't miss anonymous sources.

Do something with the information you receive. Some information begs to be attended to. If someone shares a bit of crucial information with you, perhaps with great personal anxiety and risk, you owe it to your source to tell him or her what you are going to do with the information. Then, be sure you do it, keeping them informed. It is perfectly acceptable to do nothing except think about information you receive. In fact, sometimes that is exactly the right response, but you have to be straightforward about it with your source: "Bob, thanks for telling me about this problem. I had no idea it was this serious, and I know this wasn't easy for you. Let me tell you that I'm just going to sit on this for now, but I may need to discuss it with Mr. Foster next month. Of course, I will respect your confidentiality and let you know what happens."

RATE YOUR NETWORKING SUCCESS

How do you know when your network is working for you? Here are some clues:

_____ You receive few surprises, either good or bad, because you know about most events before they occur.

_____ Your employees express support and follow through with constructive suggestions when problems need to be solved.

_____ You are among the first, not the last, to receive bad news.

_____ Your advice is routinely sought.

_____ Your sphere of contacts seems to be steadily growing.

_____ More people are sharing more information with you.

_____ You learn about future job opportunities early enough to act on them.

You know your network is in trouble when

_____ you are being surprised by good and bad news; you seem to be the last to know about significant events.

_____ you detect a decline in the flow of information.

_____ morale is deteriorating.

_____ warning signs come in the form of nonverbal actions (e.g., being left out of meetings and being "forgotten" when copies of reports and memos are distributed).

_____ the number of customer complaints increases (both outside customers and internal customers such as those in other departments).

_____ employee behaviors change.

_____ a noticeable number of people are reluctant to volunteer information.

_____ there is a lack of feedback or there is negative feedback about your own performance.

_____ you rarely hear about job opportunities "in the pipeline," or learn about them too late.

Take care of your information network and it will take care of you!

Appendix G
The Manager's Toolkit: Assertiveness and the Virtue of Saying No

Assertiveness is an intensely personal communication skill that deserves some special attention by the new manager. Imagine how this recently promoted new manager feels:

> "I'm really frustrated because I can't say 'no' to my employees or my boss. I'm too worried about losing their affection and loyalty. Then I feel worse because they probably lose respect for me when I don't stand up to them."

Many new managers are confounded with the trouble they encounter when talking to people. Somehow, they believe, all the anxiety that accompanies difficult communication was supposed to disappear after they achieved the managerial ranks.

"If I'm already in charge, why do I need to learn to be assertive?" they ask.

TO BE OR NOT TO BE: ASSERTIVENESS DEFINED

Assertiveness is a communication skill characterized by positive, direct, honest, and confident expressions about a person's own ideas, feelings, beliefs, needs, or rights. It is an interactive communication skill that signals the following to those you work with

- I don't and won't "beat around the bush" with you. I say what I mean, and mean what I say.
- I am striving to make my message clear and easy to understand. My messages are intended to be nonmanipulative; I will not play communication games that blame, confuse, or inject emotion into an otherwise rational discussion.
- I try to choose the right time to say what I have to say, taking into consideration your feelings and rights. For example, I am not insensitive to the fact that you have your own problems that make it difficult to listen to me. I will not give up my right to my say, but I will be considerate and wait for a better time.

- I believe all of us share certain rights, no matter what our position in the organization:

    > the right to express our thoughts and feelings, provided that we do not violate the rights of anyone else
    > the right to be treated with respect
    > the right to defend ourselves
    > the right to say no without feeling guilty
    > the right to ask for what we want
    > the right to make mistakes as long as we take responsibility for our actions
    > even the right to choose when to be assertive

- I am willing to listen to you when you assert your ideas, feelings, beliefs, needs, and rights. I will listen to you when you are angry or critical without reacting in a similar fashion. I will be glad to hear you give feedback as well as you take feedback.

Assertive behavior is an expression that attempts to assert your rights and enhance your message, but not at the expense of others' rights or feelings. It is a recognition that aggressive, confrontive, and passive behavior almost always confuses the message being expressed because it is dominated by emotion. It's hard to respond clearly and openly while under verbal attack!

People are not born assertive. They learn to use the skills of assertiveness the same way they learn to sing, negotiate, and speak in public. Like all skills, your assertiveness will improve with practice.

WHY IS ASSERTIVENESS AN IMPORTANT SKILL TO LEARN?

You're going to need assertiveness every day that you are a manager. You are the target of everyone else's communciation games, but you cannot allow yourself to play them in response. Your employees will try to manipulate, mislead, and misdirect you. They will lie to you, directly and by omission. They will direct their anger, frustration, anxiety, and guilt toward you, whether you deserve it or not. You will see them at their worst, so you must be at your best in order to express your message clearly, fairly, and exactly the way you mean it.

The payoffs for developing your assertiveness skills are as varied as your communication patterns. Just imagine how much easier your job will be when your employees, peers, and boss all understand you and feel they have been treated fairly in the communication process! You are certainly unleashing much more of your personal power when you assert yourself, but at the same time, you are making it possible for others to do likewise by setting the standard and providing the example for clear communication.

Utlimately, the purpose of developing a repertoire of assertive communication skills is to increase your effectiveness in professional and social situations. This purpose is based on the assumption that people are more likely to achieve their goals by letting others know what they feel, think, and want.

ASSERTIVENESS APPLIED

So, how does a person become assertive? It's simple: by becoming the most persistently fair and straightforward communicator he or she can be. *This means to DO the following:*

- describe directly and completely the situation or behavior of the people with whom you are dealing
- describe your feelings
- explain how others' comments and behaviors have affected you
- focus your comments on results and observable behavior (which you can change), not personalities (which you cannot change)
- empathize with the other person's position
- state briefly, firmly, and specifically the alternatives or changes you would like to occur
- provide feedback
- invite feedback
- listen attentively and uncritically without beginning an internal discussion with yourself
- make sure you understand each other's interpretation of a problem before moving toward a solution

It also means to NOT DO the following:

- misrepresent, withhold, or lie about information (your long-term integrity and credibility are at stake)
- manipulate via emotions, exaggerations, melodrama, or compliments
- overload with too much criticism or praise at one time
- pass out advice
- masquerade criticism or requests with compliments
- apologize unnecessarily or excessively

- send conflicting messages (your "yes" should mean yes, not "yes, but . . .")
- generalize
- evaluate the other's comments too quickly
- react immediately to criticism (explore what is meant, ask for examples)
- jump to conclusions
- take over decision-making process

If you feel you would benefit from assertiveness training, check with your human resources department, trade association, or community college for possible classes.

Appendix H
The Manager's Toolkit: Personal Development and Life-Long Learning

What's next for you? Are you taking care of your own development as well as you take care of your employees' development?

We began this book by acknowledging that you must be doing a lot of things right in order to make the change from worker to manager. Now is not the time to slow down. Now you have some of the time and resources you need to make some significant investments in yourself.

We also asserted that most of what you're going to learn about your job is going to be learned on the job, while you are doing the work of managing. You learn by observing, discussing, and finally doing the work. This is going to continue, so don't become fearful of making a mistake or two.

Here are some suggestions for building and maintaining your personal self-development plan:

Refresh and reset your goals. Get some help with your goals, either from your manager, your mentor, or a colleague. Advice and feedback from someone who has had experience with your company would be particularly helpful in pointing out opportunities and possible career paths. This person also may be able to share additional insights about the company's long-term growth strategy, which will give you important clues as to how you should prepare yourself. Advice will also help you keep your goals realistic: "Sorry, Janet—it is unlikely you can become a plant manager in less than five years."

Continue to take care of the present, and the future will take care of itself. Keep your priorities clearly in mind: Now is not the time to forget to take care of your needs as a boss, the mission of your department, or the details of your operation. The question you asked at the beginning of this book was, "Can I succeed as a manager?" Well, so far, so good, right? Now the question is, "Can I manage my success?"

Find ways to practice and develop your planning, decision making, and communication skills. Although many other types of skills are also important, these three will remain the most important far into your future. They will help you in more ways, more often, as your career progresses.

Practice managing changes. You are more than an administrator—you are a masterful change agent, leading the organization toward its prosperous future. If you can become good at this, you will be a valued contributor no matter how your job changes. Keep these tips in mind when you cause change to occur:

1. Share your excitement about the upcoming change; people need this to replace their former vision.

2. Share as much information as you can about the change; this helps some people to deal with their anxiety about the uncertainty while slowing the spread of misunderstandings and rumors.

3. Change means that choices have to be made; let others participate in those choices so that they have some ownership in the outcome.

4. Keep surprises to a minimum; communicating the plan in small, easy-to-understand steps reduces confusion and anxiety.

5. Go fast enough to keep people interested and motivated, but not so fast that uncertainty as with a "runaway train" becomes the dominant feeling.

6. Communicate your expectations for performance clearly and consistently.

7. Adopt a "can do" style for yourself, and reward others who do the same.

8. Highlight the benefits of the change as soon as they become real; let others know as soon as you can that the change is worth their extra effort.

9. If someone loses because of this change, be honest with them up front so that they can prepare and change themselves into winners, too.

10. Change only that which is necessary to change; some familiarity with past routines and habits makes it possible to adopt new routines and habits.

11. Begin planning for the next change immediately; by the time you're ready for it, you will need it, because yesterday's "new" has become today's "old."

12. Finally, overcommunicate. Never assume that you have been completely understood, par-

ticularly by those who may be resisting change for reasons of their own.

Recruit a development partner. Your development will be richer if you can give and receive support from a like-minded person in your company, or in a company like yours, who is experiencing similar challenges and satisfactions.

Cultivate your personal network. These company friends and acquaintances may last a lifetime, providing you with priceless insights, foresights, and customer and supplier introductions.

Seek feedback about your performance. You cannot get too much feedback, too often. Make sure that your perception of your contribution is shared by those important to your success.

Manage your manager. Learn what is important to your manager, then make it important to you. Does he value reports and plans? Master the word processor and give him the best reading material he's ever had. Does he always put customer service above all else? Make the customers your passion. Innovation? Frequent discussions? Group meetings? Sales promotion? It doesn't matter; every boss is entitled to his or her individual style. Your job is to take care of your boss, and that means supporting your manager's agenda. If you take care of your boss, he or she will take care of you. Knowing your boss well can save you an enormous amount of time—time that you can reinvest in your own agenda. A final word about managing your manager: Never, never let your boss be surprised with bad news that you could have delivered first.

Get results. It is your job to get results; this is why you are paid more than others. Of course, how you get results is usually as important as the outcomes; so short-term results at the expense of permanent progress is a poor bargain.

Have fun. If you do not enjoy managing, don't do it. If you do enjoy it, I wish you a full and happy career; may you always make your numbers.

Good luck! You have a great start to your career!

Index